WHAT EVERY LEADER MUST KNOW

The Essentials of Empowering Leadership

Unlocking the Secrets to Inspiring, Motivating,
and Leading with Purpose

Legacy Reference Edition

Aaron Prempeh

Purpose Givers Publications
Iowa City, Iowa, USA

1

Copyright © 2026 by Aaron Prempeh

All rights reserved.

No part of this book may be reproduced, stored in a retrieval system, or transmitted in any form or by any means — electronic, mechanical, photocopying, recording, or otherwise — without prior written permission from the copyright owner, except for brief quotations in reviews or scholarly works.

The views expressed in this work are solely those of the author and do not necessarily reflect the views of the publisher. The publisher disclaims any responsibility for such views.

ISBN (Paperback): 979-8-9944566-1-3

Published by

Purpose Givers Publications

Iowa City, Iowa, USA

Websites:

aaronprempeh.com

aaronprempehbooks.com

purposegivers.co

info@purposegivers.co

Printed in the United States of America

Table of Contents

Back Matter

DEDICATION

To all the **great leaders** who paid the price to make this world a better place. To all who are striving to develop and enhance their leadership skills and abilities to serve this generation and the generations to come.

This book is dedicated to:

Every leader who has ever doubted their capacity to rise, Every dreamer who refused to surrender to limitation, Every servant-hearted visionary committed to lifting others, And every future leader whose journey is just beginning.

May this work awaken purpose, strengthen courage, inspire service, and ignite a legacy that outlives the present generation.

Champion Remain. — Aaron Prempeh

ACKNOWLEDGMENTS

To my beloved wife and son — your unwavering support, patience, and sacrifices have been my anchor throughout this journey. Your love, encouragement, and belief in my vision have made this project possible. I am deeply grateful for the strength and inspiration you give me every day.

To the mentors and great leaders who have shaped my journey — thank you. Your guidance, wisdom, and encouragement have been invaluable. You have helped mold my perspective, strengthen my character, and refine my understanding of leadership.

To the great leadership writers who have taken the time to document their insights, experiences, and discoveries — I honor you. You have provided a wellspring of knowledge from which I have drawn inspiration and understanding for this work. Through your dedication, this book is able to carry forward wisdom that might otherwise remain inaccessible to many.

To every courageous leader who has dared to stand, serve, and transform society — this book is a tribute to you.

"Leadership is the courage to stand when others sit,

the vision to see what others miss,

and the heart to lift others higher than yourself.

When such leaders rise, history moves forward."

— Aaron Prempeh

FOREWORD

"It's wonderful when the people believe in their leader…
but it's even more wonderful when the leader believes in
the people!"
— *Unknown*

Leadership is not a solitary journey. It is a path shaped and
refined by those who have gone before us. As Isaac
Newton wisely observed, *"If I have seen further, it is by
standing on the shoulders of giants."* These giants are the
mentors, coaches, teachers, and spiritual guides who
illuminate our path with their wisdom and experience.

In the pursuit of leadership, it is essential to recognize and
follow those who exemplify integrity, loyalty, faithfulness,
discipline, determination, diligence, dedication, and
sacrifice. Scripture gives us a powerful illustration: David
transformed men who were discontented, distressed, and
indebted into mighty warriors through the skill of his
hands and the integrity of his heart. This reveals a
timeless truth — **good followership is the foundation
of great leadership.**

The lesson is clear: **Follow well to lead well.**

In this book, you will discover invaluable insights, principles,
and practical wisdom that will equip you to become the
leader you are called to be. I wholeheartedly recommend
this work to every aspiring leader, established leader, and
servant-hearted visionary who desires to grow, influence,
and leave a legacy.

May this book inspire you to lead with courage, serve with
humility, and impact generations.

Bishop Michael Hutton Wood

Author, Leadership Secrets

Founder & Senior Pastor, House of Judah Ministries (UK)

Principal, Generational Leadership Training Institute

Director, Leadership Factory International

PREFACE

Leadership is one of the most critical forces shaping organizations, communities, and nations. Yet many people step into leadership roles without clear guidance on what leadership truly is, why it matters, and how it is developed. This book exists to bridge that gap.

What Every Leader Must Know provides essential insights and practical answers about leadership, guiding you to understand why leaders are needed, what leadership truly is and is not, the importance of leadership, who a leader is, and the key aspects of leadership thinking and attitude. It explores leadership philosophy, leadership functions, character development, and the timeless truth that great leaders are made, not born.

This book serves as a leadership handbook designed to walk readers through the process of leadership development. Leadership can be defined as "the ability to influence a group toward the achievement of a vision or set of goals." Whether you manage, supervise, mentor, pastor, coach, or influence others in any capacity, this book will equip you with the principles, mindset, and skills required to meet today's leadership challenges with confidence and clarity.

The inspiration for this book was born following a leadership speaking engagement at a conference held at the Hilton Hotel in London, United Kingdom, organized by the Foundation for Leadership Excellence (FLEX). After the program, there was strong demand for my leadership materials — but I had nothing available beyond my presentation notes.

My childhood friend and cousin, Mr. Patrick Adumatta, who
attended the conference, encouraged me to document
these insights in book form, believing the message could
impact leaders far beyond that event. His encouragement
became the spark that initiated this work. Patrick, thank
you for believing in my potential.

It is my sincere hope that this book will inspire, equip, and
strengthen all who are called to lead — helping them
develop the skills, character, confidence, and competence
necessary to influence their world positively and build
lasting legacies.

Aaron Prempeh
Author, *What Every Leader Must Know*

HOW TO USE THIS BOOK

What Every Leader Must Know is designed to be more than a book to read — it is a guide to study, apply, teach, and revisit.

You may use this book in any of the following ways:

1. Personal Leadership Growth

Read one chapter at a time and reflect carefully on the KEY TAKEAWAYS, reflection questions, and action steps. Do not rush. Leadership is formed through practice, not merely through information.

2. Daily or Weekly Leadership Devotion

Use one chapter per day or per week as a leadership development focus. Read, reflect, journal, and identify one practical action to apply immediately.

3. Group Study or Leadership Training

This book can be used in churches, businesses, schools, mentoring groups, fellowships, leadership academies, and training cohorts. Each chapter contains discussion-friendly material that can be reviewed together.

4. Coaching and Mentoring Tool

Coaches, mentors, pastors, and trainers may use reflection questions and action steps to guide conversations, evaluate growth, and develop emerging leaders.

5. Reference Handbook

Because leadership challenges change with season and responsibility, this book can also serve as a reference manual. Return to specific chapters whenever you need clarity, courage, wisdom, **or direction.**

Recommended Approach

Leadership is a journey of influence, service, growth, and legacy. My prayer is that this book will not only inform you but transform you.

INTRODUCTION

Leadership determines whether families thrive, organizations grow, institutions endure, and nations rise or fall. Yet many people step into positions of responsibility without ever being taught what leadership truly is, what it demands, or how it is developed.

That gap has created a crisis of influence in homes, churches, businesses, communities, and governments.

This book was written to close that gap.

Whether you are a pastor, executive, entrepreneur, teacher, parent, coach, ministry leader, student leader, or community servant, the principles in these pages are designed to help you lead with clarity, character, courage, and purpose. Leadership is not reserved for a gifted few. It can be learned, strengthened, refined, and lived.

"Today a reader — tomorrow a leader." — W. Fusselman "The world is moving so fast these days that the man who says it can't be done is generally interrupted by someone doing it." — Harry Emerson Fosdick

Leadership is a vital force behind human progress. It shapes businesses, families, governments, ministries, communities, and nations. Two undeniable truths exist about leadership: leaders are essential, and a leadership crisis always exists—whether through a shortage of capable leaders or the presence of ineffective, corrupt, or unethical leadership.

While some individuals may display natural leadership tendencies, anyone with desire, discipline, and determination can learn to become an effective leader.

Leadership is not a gift reserved for a few; it is a capacity developed through continuous self-study, education, training, mentorship, and experience.

A common misconception is that leadership and management are the same. Though related, they are fundamentally different. This misunderstanding often causes people to underestimate the importance of intentional leadership development. This book is designed to clarify what leadership truly is, why it matters, and the essential principles every leader must know.

Leadership can be defined as the ability to influence a group toward the achievement of a vision or a set of goals. A leader possesses a clear sense of direction—an understanding of where to go and what success looks like. Yet vision alone is not enough. Leaders must communicate vision effectively and act upon it decisively.

As Jack Welch, former Chairman and CEO of General Electric, once said:
"Good business leaders create a vision, articulate the vision, passionately own the vision, and relentlessly drive it to completion."

Passion is contagious. When leaders believe deeply in their vision, others will follow. Discipline then keeps the vision on course, directing both the leader's actions and the team's efforts toward the desired outcome. The hallmark of great leadership is action—leaders do not suffer from analysis paralysis; they move forward and inspire others to do the same.

The Rotary Club's Four-Way Test provides a timeless framework for evaluating leadership decisions:

- Is it the truth?

- Is it fair to all concerned?

- Will it build goodwill and better friendships?

- Will it be beneficial to all concerned?

Leadership is universally recognized as essential—but true leadership goes beyond holding a title or position. True leaders elevate others. As John Quincy Adams wisely stated:

"If your actions inspire others to dream more, learn more, do more, and become more—you are a leader."

Despite the abundance of educated and motivated individuals in the world, many lack the knowledge and confidence to lead effectively. As a result, some avoid leadership altogether, while others struggle in leadership roles believing they simply "were not born to lead." This is a tragic misconception. Our world desperately needs good leaders—in corporations, churches, schools, homes, communities, and governments. Even parents must become effective leaders to build healthy families.

Leadership takes many forms. From CEOs to teachers, pastors to coaches, entrepreneurs to parents—leadership touches every sphere of life. One of the most defining aspects of leadership is how a leader thinks. As the saying goes:

"As a man thinks, so he becomes."

Understanding the mindset of a leader is key to unlocking effective leadership.

To illustrate this truth, consider the following story:

The Eagle Story — Discovering Your True Identity

High on a mountain sat an eagle's nest containing a single
egg. One day, a powerful wind swept the egg from the
nest, sending it rolling down the mountain into a valley
where it landed in a chicken farm. A kind hen found the
strange egg and decided to incubate it with her own.

In time, the egg hatched. The young bird looked different—
its beak, wings, and feet unlike those of the chicks around
it. The other chickens laughed at its appearance. Yet the
young eagle grew up among them, behaving like them,
believing it was one of them.

Deep within, however, the eagle carried a dream—to one day
fly beyond the farm's fence. The other chickens mocked
the idea, insisting, "You are a chicken. Chickens do not
fly."

One morning, the young bird saw a majestic eagle soaring
high above. Overcome with longing, it cried out, "How
can I fly like you?"

The great eagle descended and studied the young bird
carefully. Then it said:

"Your beak is like mine.
Your feet are like mine.
Your wings are like mine.
You are not a chicken—you are an eagle."

"Flap your wings," the eagle instructed.

With hesitation, the young bird spread its wings. Strength surged through its body. With one powerful thrust, it lifted off the ground—soaring into the sky.

In that moment, it realized the truth:

It had never been a chicken.
It had always been an eagle—born to soar.

MORAL OF THE STORY

Our environment and the opinions of others can distort our understanding of who we truly are. Many people accept limitations placed upon them by society, family, fear, or self-doubt. Yet with the right guidance, mentorship, and self-belief, we can break free from these constraints and discover our true potential.

Like the eagle, greatness already resides within you. True leaders see not only what is—but what could be.

CALL TO AWAKENING

There is a giant within you waiting to be awakened.
There is a leader within you waiting to rise.

Your generation is waiting for you.
Your family is waiting for you.
Your community is waiting for you.
Your nation is waiting for you.
The world is waiting for you.

Do not ignore the call.

Be the eagle you were born to be.

"For the earnest expectation of creation eagerly waits for the manifestation of the sons of God." — Romans 8:19 (KJV)

PART I — THE ESSENCE OF LEADERSHIP
A leader awakens purpose.

CHAPTER 1 — The Call to Leadership

Introduction

The journey to leadership often begins with a sense of calling — a deep inner realization that one is meant to guide, influence, and inspire others. This call is not merely about assuming a position of authority; it is about recognizing a responsibility to serve, to make a difference, and to lead people toward a shared vision.

Every great leader's story begins with a moment of awakening. Some hear the call quietly through inner conviction. Others are thrust into leadership by circumstance. But in every case, leadership begins when purpose meets responsibility.

This chapter explores what it means to be called to leadership, the motivations behind this calling, how individuals respond to it, and the lasting impact of answering the call.

"It's wonderful when the people believe in their leader... but it's even more wonderful when the leader believes in the people!"
— *Unknown*

Leadership Story

The Unexpected Call

A young professional was comfortable in his role — meeting expectations, performing assigned duties, and avoiding additional responsibility. Leadership was not something he actively pursued.

One day, his supervisor resigned unexpectedly, and he was asked to step in temporarily.

He hesitated.

He felt unprepared, uncertain, and questioned whether he was capable of leading others. But as the days unfolded, something shifted. His team began to look to him for direction. Decisions needed to be made. Problems required solutions.

In that moment, he realized something profound:

Leadership is not about readiness — it is about responsibility.

He chose to step forward. He listened, learned, adapted, and acted. What began as a temporary assignment became a defining moment of leadership.

Leadership Insight

Leadership often finds you before you feel ready. The call to leadership is rarely convenient — but it is always purposeful.

Application

Do not wait until you feel fully prepared. Step forward when responsibility calls. Growth happens in motion, not in hesitation.

1. Understanding the Call to Leadership

The call to leadership is an internal drive that compels an individual to step forward and take responsibility for guiding others. It is often the alignment of personal passion, experience, and a recognized need in the world around them.

This calling is deeply personal. It may emerge from adversity, injustice, opportunity, or a vision of something better. True leadership calling is not about self-promotion; it is about purposeful contribution.

1.1 The Inner Voice

For many leaders, the call begins as an inner voice — a quiet but persistent conviction that they are meant to do more. It may arise from personal struggles, empathy for others, or a desire to solve problems.

At first, the voice whispers. Over time, as confidence and clarity grow, the voice becomes a compelling directive: *Step forward. Lead.*

1.2 External Influences

Sometimes the call comes through external affirmation. Mentors, role models, family members, or community leaders may recognize leadership potential before the individual does. Significant events, crises, or urgent challenges can also act as catalysts that push a person into leadership.

Many leaders discover their calling not in comfort, but in moments when leadership is needed most.

2. Motivations Behind the Call

Understanding why one desires to lead is essential for remaining grounded in purpose.

2.1 Desire to Serve

The greatest leaders are driven by service. They see leadership as a platform to uplift others, solve problems, and improve lives. Service-driven leadership earns trust and loyalty.

2.2 Passion for Change

Some leaders are called by vision. They see a better future and feel compelled to challenge the status quo. Their passion fuels resilience and courage.

2.3 Sense of Duty

Others are motivated by responsibility. They feel morally or spiritually obligated to lead when others need guidance. This sense of duty often produces steady and dependable leaders.

2.4 Recognition of Potential

Some respond to the call when they realize they possess gifts, knowledge, or experience that can benefit others. Leadership becomes stewardship of ability.

3. Responding to the Call

Recognizing the call is only the beginning. The true test is response.

3.1 Self-Reflection

Effective leaders begin with introspection. They ask:

- Why am I called to lead?

- What values guide me?

- What impact do I desire to make?

Clarity of purpose precedes clarity of leadership.

3.2 Developing Leadership Capacity

Leadership requires preparation. Aspiring leaders commit to learning, mentorship, experience, and continuous improvement. Calling without competence leads to frustration; competence aligned with calling produces influence.

3.3 Taking Action

Leadership is ultimately expressed through action. Those who answer the call step forward despite fear, uncertainty, or discomfort. Courage is the first visible evidence of leadership.

4. Challenges of the Call

The path of leadership is rewarding — but not easy.

4.1 Overcoming Self-Doubt

Even great leaders wrestle with insecurity. Overcoming self-doubt requires belief in purpose greater than fear.

4.2 Facing Resistance

Leadership challenges comfort. Resistance is inevitable. Leaders must learn to stand firm while building understanding.

4.3 Managing Expectations

Leaders balance ambition with patience, excellence with realism, and urgency with wisdom.

5. The Impact of Answering the Call

Leaders who respond to their calling transform environments.

5.1 Inspiring Others

Purpose-driven leaders ignite belief in others. Their conviction becomes contagious.

5.2 Driving Positive Change

Every movement, innovation, and transformation begins with someone who answered the call to lead.

5.3 Leaving a Legacy

True leadership is measured not by achievements alone, but by the lives changed and leaders raised.

6. Conclusion

The call to leadership is an invitation to purpose. It begins in the heart, is shaped through preparation, and is fulfilled through service. While the journey includes challenge and sacrifice, it also offers the opportunity to influence generations and shape history.

Those who answer the call do not merely lead — they light the way for others to follow. This call to leadership now leads us to understand what leadership truly is at its core.

KEY TAKEAWAYS

- Leadership begins with a sense of calling

- Calling aligns purpose with responsibility

- Leadership requires preparation and courage

- Resistance and doubt are part of the journey

- True leadership impact is measured in legacy

REFLECTION QUESTIONS

1. When did I first sense my call to leadership?

2. What leadership responsibilities have I avoided?

3. Where do I feel God or purpose calling me to lead?

4. What motivates my desire to lead?

5. What fears hold me back from stepping forward fully?

6. What leadership skills must I now develop?

7. What legacy do I want my leadership to leave?

ACTION STEPS

1. Write your personal leadership calling statement.

2. Identify one mentor to guide your leadership growth.

3. Begin a leadership learning plan this month.

4. Volunteer to lead one small initiative this week.

5. Reflect weekly on your leadership progress.

Closing Thought

Leadership begins with a call — but it is sustained by a decision. Answer the call and commit to the journey.

CHAPTER 2 — The Concept of Leadership

Introduction

Every meaningful journey begins with a calling. Once that call is recognized, the next essential step is understanding what leadership truly is. Leadership has guided human progress across generations, yet it remains one of the most misunderstood forces in society. To lead effectively, we must first understand the concept that shapes all leadership practice.

Leadership has been central to human progress since the dawn of civilization. From tribal chiefs and kings to modern executives, pastors, presidents, and community leaders, it has shaped societies, organizations, and nations. Yet despite its universal presence, leadership remains a complex and multi-dimensional concept — influenced by personality, culture, context, and purpose.

This chapter examines the concept of leadership by exploring its definitions, major theories, core elements, and evolving nature. Understanding these foundations provides the essential framework for becoming an effective and influential leader.

1. Defining Leadership

Leadership can be broadly defined as the process of influencing people to work willingly toward the achievement of a shared goal. At its core, leadership is influence toward a shared purpose.

In practice, leadership goes beyond position; it is demonstrated through action, responsibility, and consistency.

For example, individuals without formal authority can still lead by shaping decisions and encouraging others.

True leadership is measured not by title, but by impact. It involves guiding, motivating, and empowering individuals or groups to move from vision to reality. Leadership is relational, situational, and dynamic, expressed through influence rather than position.

Anyone, regardless of formal authority, can exercise leadership by influencing attitudes, behaviors, and outcomes.

2. Key Theories of Leadership

Over decades, scholars and practitioners have developed theories to explain how leadership works. Each theory provides valuable insight into different dimensions of leadership effectiveness.

2.1 Trait Theory

Trait theory suggests that effective leaders possess inherent personal characteristics that distinguish them from non-leaders. Common leadership traits include intelligence, confidence, integrity, determination, and sociability.

Insight:
While traits contribute to leadership potential, leadership

effectiveness is not determined by traits alone. Skills, discipline, and experience also matter.

2.2 Behavioral Theory

Behavioral theory focuses on what leaders do rather than who they are. It proposes that leadership behaviors can be learned and developed.

Two primary behavior styles are:

- **Task-Oriented Behavior** — Focused on planning, structure, and goal achievement

- **People-Oriented Behavior** — Focused on relationships, support, and engagement

Effective leaders learn to balance both dimensions.

2.3 Situational Leadership Theory

Situational leadership theory asserts that no single leadership style is universally effective. Leaders must adapt their approach based on the needs of followers and the demands of the environment.

For example:

- High direction during crises

- High collaboration during stable growth

Adaptability defines leadership maturity.

2.4 Transformational Leadership Theory

Transformational leadership focuses on inspiring and elevating followers beyond ordinary expectations. Transformational leaders:

- Create compelling vision

- Stimulate innovation

- Develop followers

- Drive positive change

This contrasts with **Transactional Leadership**, which emphasizes rewards and performance exchange.

3. Core Elements of Leadership

Effective leadership rests on several interconnected elements.

3.1 Vision

Vision provides direction and meaning. Leaders paint a clear picture of the future and align people toward it.

3.2 Communication

Leadership rises or falls on communication. Leaders must speak clearly, listen actively, and create understanding.

3.3 Influence

Effective leadership relies on influence rather than force — leaders inspire people to contribute willingly through trust, credibility, and shared purpose.

3.4 Decision-Making

Leaders make timely and informed decisions, especially under uncertainty. Decisiveness builds confidence.

3.5 Emotional Intelligence

Self-awareness, self-control, empathy, and social skills enable leaders to navigate relationships and pressure effectively.

4. The Importance of Context in Leadership

Leadership never operates in a vacuum. Culture, industry, team maturity, and situational demands shape leadership practice. What succeeds in one context may fail in another. Wise leaders read their environment before they act.

5. Leadership vs. Management

Though closely related, leadership and management serve different functions.

- **Leadership** sets vision, inspires people, and drives change.

- **Management** plans, organizes, and controls processes.

- Organizations thrive when both are present in balance.

6. The Evolution of Leadership Concepts

Traditional leadership emphasized command and control. Modern leadership emphasizes collaboration, empowerment, inclusion, and ethical responsibility. Globalization and digital transformation now demand agility, emotional intelligence, and cross-cultural competence from leaders.

7. Conclusion

Leadership is both an art and a science — the ability to guide people toward a shared future with clarity, purpose, and impact. It blends vision, adaptability, and character. As environments evolve, so must leaders. Those who understand the foundations of leadership position themselves not only to grow, but to inspire others and create lasting influence. This foundation prepares us to now explore what leadership truly is in practical terms.

KEY TAKEAWAYS

- Leadership is influence directed toward a shared purpose.

- Leadership theories explain different dimensions of effectiveness

- Vision, communication, and emotional intelligence are core elements

- Context determines leadership style

- Leadership and management are complementary

- Modern leadership emphasizes empowerment and adaptability

REFLECTION QUESTIONS

1. How do I personally define leadership?

2. Which leadership theory best describes my current style?

3. How well do I adapt my leadership skills to different situations?

4. Do I prioritize vision, people, or tasks — and is my balance healthy?

5. How strong is my emotional intelligence in leadership interactions?

ACTION STEPS

1. Write your personal leadership definition.

2. Identify one leadership theory to study deeper this month.

3. Ask two colleagues how they experience your leadership.

4. Practice active listening in your next meeting.

5. Clarify and communicate a vision for your team this week.

Closing Thought

Leadership is not defined by position, but by influence. When you understand this, you begin to lead with purpose.

CHAPTER 3 — What Is Leadership?

Introduction

Leadership is a word used everywhere — in business, ministry, politics, education, and family life. Yet few stop asking what it means beyond titles and authority. Before anyone can lead well, they must understand what leadership truly is at its core.

Leadership has been defined and redefined across generations. From military generals to business executives, pastors, presidents, and community organizers, leaders are individuals who inspire, guide, and influence others toward shared goals. But leadership is more than a title, a position, or a personality trait — it is a force that shapes people, organizations, and nations.

This chapter explores the meaning of leadership through key definitions, characteristics, real-world examples, and common misconceptions — providing a practical and timeless understanding of what it truly means to lead.

1. Defining Leadership

1.1 Leadership as Influence

"Leadership is influence — nothing more, nothing less." — John Maxwell

At its core, leadership operates through influence — the ability to shape direction, inspire action, and guide others. This influence is not based on coercion or manipulation but on inspiration and alignment of vision.

Dwight D. Eisenhower further explains:

"Leadership is the art of getting someone else to do
something you want done because he wants to do it."

True leadership aligns the leader's vision with the follower's
motivation.

Example:
Mahatma Gandhi's leadership during India's
independence movement demonstrated leadership as
influence. By aligning millions around a nonviolent vision,
he mobilized a nation without formal authority.

1.2 Leadership as a Social Process

Leadership is also a social process in which one person enlists
the cooperation and commitment of others to
accomplish shared objectives.

Alan Keith of Genentech observed:

"Leadership is ultimately about creating a way for people to
contribute to making something extraordinary happen."

This definition emphasizes collaboration, shared ownership,
and collective effort.

Example:
Nelson Mandela united divided communities in South
Africa by fostering shared purpose, reconciliation, and
collective participation in nation-building.

1.3 Leadership as Vision and Action

Warren Bennis offers a holistic definition:

"Leadership is a function of knowing yourself, having a
vision that is well communicated, building trust among
colleagues, and taking effective action."

Leadership therefore requires:

- Self-awareness

- Vision

- Trust-building

- Execution

Example:
Steve Jobs exemplified leadership as vision and action. His clear vision, persuasive communication, and relentless execution transformed Apple into a global innovation leader.

2. The Nature of Leadership

2.1 Leadership as Inspiration

Leadership is the ability to inspire people to accomplish meaningful goals. Leaders model commitment, courage, and belief. They challenge the status quo and invite others to pursue greater possibilities.

Example:
Dr. Martin Luther King Jr. inspired a nation through vision, conviction, and moral courage, advancing civil rights through hope and unity.

2.2 Leadership as Direction

Leaders set direction. They help people see what lies ahead and guide them toward it — especially during uncertainty.

Example:
Winston Churchill provided direction and resolve to Britain during World War II, transforming fear into determination through clarity of purpose.

2.3 Leadership and Followers

Leadership cannot exist without followers. John Maxwell reminds us: "He who thinks he is leading, and no one is following, is only taking a walk."

Leadership is measured not by intention, but by willing followership.

Example:

Mother Teresa's leadership was evidenced by devoted followers inspired by her life of service to the poorest of the poor.

3. The Impact of Leadership

3.1 Leadership for Good or for Harm

Leadership is powerful — and power can be used constructively or destructively. Ethical leadership builds societies; unethical leadership destroys them.

Example:

Adolf Hitler used influence destructively, demonstrating why integrity and morality are essential in leadership.

3.2 Leadership in Action — Historical Example

Before World War II, Winston Churchill warned Britain about the threat of Nazi Germany. Though initially ignored, his conviction proved correct. When crisis came, Churchill's foresight and resilience positioned him to lead Britain through its darkest hour.

This illustrates that leadership often means standing alone before others see the truth.

4. Myths and Misconceptions About Leadership

Myth 1: Leaders Are Born, Not Made

Warren Bennis dispels this myth:

"Leaders are made rather than born."

Leadership is learned through growth, experience, and
discipline.

Myth 2: Leadership Requires Charisma

Charisma helps — but character, consistency, and
competence matter more.

Myth 3: Leadership Is About Position

Titles may grant authority, but only influence earns
followership.

Myth 4: Leadership Is About Control

True leadership empowers rather than controls.

Myth 5: Education Equals Leadership

Education informs leadership — but wisdom, experience,
and emotional intelligence develop it.

5. Conclusion

Leadership is influence directed toward a shared purpose,
expressed through vision, inspiration, and action. It is not
defined by title, charisma, or control, but by the ability to
mobilize people toward meaningful goals with integrity
and courage.

Leadership can be learned, refined, and strengthened. Its true
measure is found in the lives changed, the missions
advanced, and the leaders raised in its wake.

This understanding prepares us to explore, in the next section, the **Essence of Leadership** — the foundational qualities that distinguish great leaders from average ones. Understanding what leadership is now leads us to explore why leadership is essential in every sphere of life.

KEY TAKEAWAYS

- Leadership is influence directed toward a shared purpose.

- Leadership is relational and social.

- Vision and action define effective leadership.

- Followers validate leadership.

- Integrity determines leadership impact.

- Leadership skills can be developed.

REFLECTION QUESTIONS

1. Which definition of leadership resonates most with me?

2. How do I influence others?

3. Do people follow me willingly or only by obligation?

4. How do I ensure my leadership remains ethical?

5. What leadership myth have I personally believed?

ACTION STEPS

1. Write your personal definition of leadership.

2. Ask someone how they experience your influence.

3. Identify one leadership behavior to strengthen this week.

4. Practice inspiring someone toward a shared goal.

5. Reflect weekly on your leadership growth.

Closing Thought

Leadership is not something you claim — it is something you demonstrate through consistent action and impact.

CHAPTER 4 — Why Are Leaders Needed?

Introduction

Understanding leadership is only part of the journey. The next question naturally arises: Why does leadership matter so much? History, organizations, and communities all reveal the same truth — where leadership is strong, progress follows; where it is absent, confusion prevails.

Why are leaders needed?

Leadership is not optional in human society. Every organization, community, and nation requires leadership to move forward. Without leadership, vision fades, unity breaks, progress stalls, and confusion grows. Leaders are the stabilizing and mobilizing force that transforms potential into achievement.

This chapter explores the fundamental reasons leaders are indispensable — providing vision, building unity, driving innovation, sustaining resilience, developing people, and upholding integrity.

1. Providing Vision and Direction

One of the primary reasons leaders are needed is to provide vision and direction. Every group requires clarity about where it is going and how it will get there. Leaders define the destination and chart the course.

1.1 Setting Vision

Leaders see what others do not yet see. They articulate a compelling picture of the future that inspires belief and commitment. Vision becomes the guiding light that keeps teams focused during uncertainty and challenge.

1.2 Aligning the Team

Once vision is established, leaders align people, roles, and resources toward achieving it. They ensure that each person understands their contribution to the larger mission, creating unity of purpose.

2. Fostering Collaboration and Teamwork

Complex goals cannot be achieved alone. Leaders bring people together, build trust, and create environments where cooperation thrives.

2.1 Building Strong Relationships

Leaders foster respect, trust, and open communication. When people feel valued, they contribute more fully and engage more deeply.

2.2 Encouraging Collaboration

Effective leaders break down silos, encourage knowledge-sharing, and create opportunities for collective problem-solving. Collaboration multiplies capability.

3. Inspiring Innovation and Leading Change

Progress depends on innovation. Without leadership, organizations become stagnant and unable to adapt.

3.1 Challenging the Status Quo

Leaders encourage creativity, experimentation, and continuous improvement. They reframe change as opportunity rather than threat.

3.2 Leading Through Change

During transitions — technological, structural, or cultural —
leaders provide clarity, reassurance, and steady guidance
that prevents fear from paralyzing progress.

4. Ensuring Stability and Resilience

In times of crisis and uncertainty, leadership becomes even
more critical.

4.1 Maintaining Stability in Crisis

Strong leaders remain calm under pressure, make decisive
choices, and provide clear direction. Their composure
stabilizes those they lead.

4.2 Building Organizational Resilience

Leaders anticipate risk, prepare contingencies, and build
cultures of adaptability. Resilient organizations recover
quickly and emerge stronger.

5. Nurturing Talent and Developing Future Leaders

Great leaders think beyond today — they build tomorrow's
leadership.

5.1 Mentoring and Coaching

Leaders invest in developing skills, confidence, and capacity in
others. This multiplies leadership across the organization.

5.2 Creating a Leadership Pipeline

Succession planning ensures continuity. Leaders identify high-
potential individuals and prepare them for future
responsibility.

6. Upholding Ethics and Integrity

Leadership without integrity becomes dangerous. Ethical leadership safeguards trust and credibility.

6.1 Setting Ethical Standards

Leaders model honesty, fairness, and principled decision-making. People follow what leaders practice more than what they say.

6.2 Promoting a Culture of Integrity

Transparent communication, accountability, and justice create environments where trust flourishes and misconduct declines.

7. The Importance of Wise Leadership

Scripture affirms the necessity of wise leadership:

"Where there is no counsel, the people fall; but in the multitude of counsellors there is safety."
— Proverbs 11:14 (KJV)

"Without wise leadership, a nation falls; there is safety in having many advisers." — Proverbs 11:14 (NLT)

Wise leaders seek counsel, listen well, and make informed decisions. Wisdom protects organizations and communities from unnecessary failure.

8. Trust and Integrity in Leadership

In recent years, trust in leadership has declined due to corruption, dishonesty, and abuse of power. Society is longing for leaders who are credible, ethical, and dependable.

The most successful organizations — in business,
government, churches, schools, and communities — owe
their progress to trustworthy leaders.

As Coach Jerry Yeagley observed:

"Because I understand how important leaders are to the
success of the team, I've worked hard at selecting
captains and helping them develop leadership qualities
that matter."

9. **Leadership as a Unifying Force**

Without leadership, groups drift toward division because
people see problems differently and pursue competing
solutions. Leaders align effort, unify vision, and harness
collective strength toward common goals.

Leadership transforms disagreement into direction and
diversity into synergy.

10. **Conclusion**

Leaders are indispensable. They provide vision, unify effort,
inspire innovation, sustain resilience, develop future
leaders, and uphold moral standards. Without leadership,
organizations and societies struggle to navigate
complexity, adapt to change, or realize their potential.

As the world grows more uncertain and interconnected, the
need for capable, ethical, and visionary leaders has never
been greater.

This understanding now prepares us to continue exploring
the **Essence of Leadership** in the chapters ahead.
Recognizing the importance of leadership now brings us
to examine where leadership is most needed.

KEY TAKEAWAYS

- Leaders provide vision and direction

- Leaders build unity and collaboration

- Leaders drive innovation and guide change

- Leaders sustain stability in crisis

- Leaders develop future leadership

- Integrity and wisdom define trustworthy leadership

REFLECTION QUESTIONS

1. How do I provide vision to those I lead?

2. Do people experience me as a unifying force?

3. How do I handle change and uncertainty?

4. What am I doing to develop future leaders?

5. How do I demonstrate integrity in my decisions?

ACTION STEPS

1. Clarify and write your current leadership vision.

2. Strengthen one key relationship this week.

3. Encourage one new idea from your team.

4. Identify one emerging leader to mentor.

5. Evaluate one recent decision for ethical alignment.

Closing Thought

Where there is no leadership, there is confusion. Where
leadership rises, direction and purpose follow.

CHAPTER 5 — Where Is Leadership Needed?

Introduction

Leadership does not belong to boardrooms alone. It touches every environment where people gather for purpose. From homes to nations, classrooms to corporations, leadership determines whether people rise or remain stuck.

Where is leadership needed?

The answer is simple — **everywhere**. From sports fields to boardrooms, from classrooms to government offices, from homes to houses of worship — leadership determines whether groups flourish or fail. Wherever people gather for a shared purpose, leadership is required to provide direction, unity, and momentum.

This chapter explores the key domains where leadership is indispensable and the unique impact it creates in each sphere.

1. Leadership in Sports Teams

Chuck Noll, four-time Super Bowl–winning coach, observed:

"On every team, there is a core group that sets the tone for everyone else. If the tone is positive, you have half the battle won. If it is negative, you are beaten before you ever walk on the field."

Leadership in sports is not only about tactics or talent — it is about tone, mindset, discipline, and unity.

Coaches, captains, and senior players shape morale, commitment, and performance. Roy Williams, National Championship coach, affirmed:

"Leadership is extremely important. I tell every team that it's the seniors' team. If they lead well, we're going to have a great year."

Strong sports leadership builds teamwork, perseverance, and a winning culture. Without leadership, even the most gifted team collapses under pressure.

2. Leadership in Government and Public Service

Nations rise or fall based on leadership quality. Courageous leaders are needed to confront corruption, injustice, economic instability, and social division.

Public leaders set policy, inspire unity, protect rights, and guide national vision. In times of crisis, leadership decisions determine whether nations recover or decline.

Effective governmental leadership builds trust, accountability, and hope — the foundations of national progress.

3. Leadership in Education

Schools are training grounds for future leaders. Educational leadership shapes minds, values, and aspirations.

Teachers, principals, and policymakers create environments where learning thrives, curiosity grows, and potential is unlocked. Educational leaders must manage resources, maintain standards, support students, and prepare youth for a changing world.

Without leadership in education, societies lose their future.

4. Leadership in Business and Corporations

In business, leadership drives innovation, productivity, culture, and sustainability.

Corporate leaders define vision, align teams, navigate uncertainty, and build ethical workplaces. During economic turbulence, leadership steadies organizations through wise strategy and decisive action.

Great business leaders do not only grow profits — they grow people, culture, and long-term impact.

5. Leadership in Families and Communities

Leadership begins at home. Parents and guardians are children's first experience of leadership — shaping character, values, and responsibility.

Strong family leadership builds stable communities. Community leaders unite people, advocate for local needs, and foster social cooperation.

Healthy societies are built on healthy family and community leadership.

6. Leadership in Religious Institutions

Faith institutions provide moral and spiritual guidance. Religious leaders nurture faith, counsel individuals, address social issues, and promote peace.

They serve as moral compasses in times of confusion and uncertainty, strengthening communities through shared values and purpose.

7. Leadership in Clubs and Organizations

Professional associations, charities, and social organizations
rely on leadership to coordinate activity, engage members,
and fulfill mission.

Leaders create belonging, opportunity, and impact. Without
leadership, organizations lose direction and dissolve.

8. Leadership is Needed Everywhere People Gather

Wherever people come together for shared purposes,
leadership is required. It aligns effort, resolves conflict,
mobilizes potential, and multiplies success.

9. Conclusion

Leadership is needed in every sphere of human activity. It
shapes performance in sports, direction in government,
excellence in education, success in business, stability in
families, morality in faith institutions, and unity in
communities.

As global challenges grow more complex, the demand for
courageous, ethical, and visionary leaders becomes even
greater. Leadership is not merely a position — it is
responsibility, service, and influence in action. Seeing
where leadership is needed now leads us to understand
the importance and impact of leadership.

KEY TAKEAWAYS

- Leadership is needed wherever people gather

- It sets tone, direction, and unity

- Different domains require different leadership expressions

- Strong leadership builds thriving societies

- Leadership begins at home and extends globally

REFLECTION QUESTIONS

1. In which spheres do I currently exercise leadership?

2. Where am I being called to expand my leadership influence?

3. How do I adjust my leadership style in different environments?

4. Which leadership domain challenges me most?

5. How can I lead more effectively in my family or community?

ACTION STEPS

1. Identify one leadership domain you want to strengthen.

2. Observe an effective leader in that domain this week.

3. Apply one new leadership behavior in your daily interactions.

4. Encourage leadership development in someone close to you.

5. Reflect weekly on leadership lessons learned.

Closing Thought

Leadership is needed everywhere — because influence shapes every environment you enter.

CHAPTER 6 — The Importance of Leadership

Introduction

If leadership is needed everywhere, then its importance cannot be overstated. Leadership is the invisible force that shapes culture, directs movement, and turns vision into reality.

Why is leadership so important?

Leadership is the cornerstone of success in any organization — whether a sports team, business, non-profit institution, government body, family, or community. Where leadership is strong, progress follows. Where leadership is absent or weak, stagnation and failure soon appear.

This chapter explores the indispensable role leadership plays across key domains and the consequences that follow when leadership is present — or missing.

1. Leadership in Sports Teams

Legendary coach Pat Summitt said:

"You won't win consistently without good team leadership. You've got to have players who buy into your system, demand the best from themselves and their teammates, and hold each other accountable."

Sports leadership is not only about strategy — it is about culture, mindset, and unity.

Coaches, captains, and senior players establish standards, discipline, and belief. Mike Krzyzewski added:

"Talent is important. But the single most important ingredient after talent is internal leadership."

Without leadership, non-profits lose focus and sustainability. With leadership, they transform communities. Without leadership, talent collapses under pressure. With leadership, ordinary teams achieve extraordinary results.

2. Leadership in Business and Management

In business, leadership drives vision, innovation, and performance.

Effective leaders make strategic decisions, inspire employees, build positive culture, and align people with corporate mission. They recognize strengths, address weaknesses, and unlock potential.

Leadership in business is not command — it is inspiration with accountability. Companies with strong leadership thrive in competitive markets. Companies without it drift toward decline.

3. Leadership in Times of Crisis and Change

When uncertainty rises, leadership matters most.

People look to leaders for clarity, confidence, and direction. Effective crisis leaders make decisive choices, communicate honestly, and stabilize emotions. They solve immediate problems while protecting long-term future.

During change — technological, structural, or cultural — leaders guide transitions, reduce fear, and sustain momentum.

Change tests leadership. Leadership transforms change into opportunity.

4. Leadership in Non-Profit Organizations

Non-profit leadership aligns mission with action.

Leaders inspire donors, volunteers, and staff. They steward resources wisely, uphold ethics, and keep purpose central, and transform communities and lives.

5. Leadership in Families and Communities

Leadership begins at home. Parents are a child's first leaders — shaping values, discipline, and confidence.

Strong family leadership produces stable communities. Community leaders mobilize people, address shared problems, and strengthen social bonds.

Where family and community leadership is weak, societies weaken. Where it is strong, societies flourish.

6. The Consequences of Poor Leadership

The absence of leadership is as powerful as its presence — but in destructive ways.

Without leadership:

- Vision disappears
- Morale declines
- Progress slows
- Conflict rises
- Opportunities are missed

In business, poor leadership creates toxic culture and high turnover. In communities, it produces disorder and disunity. In nations, it leads to instability.

7. Conclusion: The Indispensable Role of Leadership

Coach Mike Candrea summarized it well:

"Our team will go as far as our leaders are willing to take us."

Leadership is the backbone of every successful endeavor. It unites people toward shared goals, inspires innovation, sustains resilience, and multiplies human potential.

As global challenges grow more complex, the demand for strong, ethical, and visionary leadership becomes greater than ever. Leadership is not merely position — it is responsibility and service in action. Understanding the importance of leadership now prepares us to explore the foundation of all leadership — self-leadership.

KEY TAKEAWAYS

- Leadership determines success or failure.

- Talent without leadership collapses.

- Leadership matters most during crisis and change.

- Strong leadership builds thriving organizations.

- Poor leadership produces stagnation.

- Leadership is influence in action, directed toward a shared purpose.

REFLECTION QUESTIONS

1. Where have I seen leadership make the greatest difference?

2. How do I lead when pressure rises?

3. Do people feel inspired or merely managed under my leadership?

4. How do I develop leadership skills in others?

5. What leadership habits must I strengthen now?

ACTION STEPS

1. Observe a strong leader and note their behaviors.

2. Identify one leadership habit to improve this week.

3. Encourage accountability within your team or family.

4. Practice clear communication in your next meeting.

5. Reflect weekly on leadership growth.

Closing Thought

Leadership is the difference between potential and progress. Without it, vision remains unrealized.

PART II — THE CORE OF LEADERSHIP

A leader masters self before leading others.

CHAPTER 7 — The Power of Self-Leadership

Introduction

Before anyone can lead others effectively, they must first master self-leadership — the foundation of all leadership. Self-leadership is the ability to take responsibility for your life, your choices, your mindset, and your actions. It determines your discipline, credibility, resilience, and consistency — the very qualities others look for in a leader.

This chapter explores the meaning of self-leadership, its importance, and practical strategies for developing and practicing it daily.

Leadership Story

Leading Myself Before Leading Others

There were moments in my journey when I desired to lead others — but I came to a difficult realization: I had not fully mastered leading myself.

Discipline was inconsistent. Time management needed improvement. Emotional control required maturity. Personal growth demanded honesty.

I discovered that leadership is first internal before it becomes external.

Before you influence others, you must learn to govern your own thoughts, habits, and decisions. I began to focus on building discipline, clarity, and intentional daily habits.

As I grew internally, something changed externally — my leadership influence became stronger, clearer, and more effective.

The breakthrough was simple but powerful:

Leadership begins within.

Leadership Insight

You cannot effectively lead others beyond the level at which you lead yourself.

Application

Develop daily disciplines:

- Manage your time intentionally

- Strengthen your mindset

- Practice self-reflection

- Commit to personal growth

Mastery of self is the foundation of leadership influence.

1. Understanding Self-Leadership

Self-leadership is the process of influencing yourself to achieve personal goals, sustain motivation, and align behavior with values and purpose. It means being proactive rather than reactive — choosing intentional action over impulsive reaction.

Self-leaders do not wait to be managed. They manage themselves.

1.1 Components of Self-Leadership

Self-Awareness

Understanding your strengths, weaknesses, values, emotions, and triggers.

Self-Motivation

The ability to inspire yourself to act, persist, and progress despite obstacles.

Self-Discipline

The capacity to control impulses and remain focused on long-term objectives.

Self-Regulation

Managing thoughts, emotions, and behaviors in alignment with values and goals.

Together, these components create personal mastery — the first requirement of leadership mastery.

1.2 Why Self-Leadership Matters

Self-leadership enables individuals to:

- Develop clarity of purpose
- Make value-based decisions

- Build resilience in adversity

- Maintain consistency under pressure

- Commit to lifelong growth

  You cannot lead others beyond the level at which you lead yourself.

2. Developing Self-Leadership

Self-leadership is cultivated — not inherited. It requires intentional growth.

2.1 Setting Personal Goals

SMART Goals

Specific, Measurable, Achievable, Relevant, and Time-bound goals provide direction.

Personal Vision and Mission

Writing a personal vision and mission clarifies life purpose and decision filters.

2.2 Building Self-Awareness

Journaling

Capturing thoughts and experiences reveals patterns and motivations.

Mindfulness Practices

Meditation and reflection sharpen emotional awareness and focus.

Feedback from Others: Trusted voices reveal blind spots and growth opportunities.

2.3 Enhancing Self-Motivation

Find Your Why Purpose fuels perseverance.

Positive Affirmation Healthy self-talk strengthens confidence.

Celebrating Progress Small wins reinforce momentum.

2.4 Cultivating Self-Discipline

Time Management Prioritizing what matters most builds control of daily actions.

Avoiding Distractions Focus protects productivity.

Accountability Partnerships Shared commitment strengthens follow-through.

3. Practicing Self-Leadership Daily

3.1 Taking Initiative

Self-leaders act before being asked. They create opportunities rather than wait for permission.

Continuous Learning keeps self-leaders relevant, adaptable, and growing.

3.2 Values-Based Decision-Making

Self-leaders filter choices through values, not impulses.

They take **calculated risks** that stretch capacity and confidence.

3.3 Managing Stress and Adversity

Self-leaders build resilience by reframing challenges as growth opportunities.

They practice stress-management disciplines to maintain balance.

3.4 Reflecting and Adjusting

Regular reflection measures progress and recalibrates direction.

Adaptability keeps leaders aligned with evolving circumstances.

4. The Impact of Self-Leadership

Self-leadership transforms both personal life and external leadership.

4.1 Empowering Others

Leaders who master themselves inspire others by example.

They naturally become mentors who multiply leadership.

4.2 Achieving Personal Fulfillment

Alignment between values and actions produces meaning, peace, and satisfaction.

Self-leadership harmonizes personal and professional life.

4.3 Contributing to Organizational Success

Self-leaders bring:

- Higher productivity
- Strong accountability
- Positive culture
- Continuous improvement

Organizations rise or fall with the level of self-leadership within them.

5. Conclusion: The Journey of Self-Leadership

Self-leadership is a lifelong journey of self-discovery, discipline, and growth. It requires courage to examine oneself honestly and commitment to improve continuously.

When you learn to lead yourself, you earn the credibility to lead others. Mastering self-leadership now leads us to explore who a leader truly is.

Great leadership always begins with self-leadership.

KEY TAKEAWAYS

- Self-leadership is the foundation of all leadership
- You cannot lead others beyond your self-leadership level
- Self-awareness, discipline, and motivation are core
- Self-leadership requires intentional practice
- Self-leadership multiplies external leadership impact

REFLECTION QUESTIONS

1. In what areas do I lead myself well?
2. Where do I lack self-discipline?
3. What values guide my daily decisions?
4. How do I respond under pressure?
5. What self-leadership habit will I strengthen next?

ACTION STEPS

1. Write your personal vision statement.

2. Identify one self-discipline habit to develop this week.

3. Begin a daily reflection journal.

4. Choose an accountability partner.

5. Set one SMART personal growth goal.

Closing Thought

If you cannot lead yourself, you cannot lead others. Leadership always begins within.

CHAPTER 8 — Who Is a Leader?

Introduction

Once self-leadership is understood, a deeper question emerges: Who truly qualifies as a leader? Is leadership defined by position, personality, or something deeper rooted in character, influence, vision, and impact?

A true leader is not defined by position, but by the ability to inspire, guide, and mobilize others toward meaningful purpose. This chapter clarifies who a leader is by exploring defining qualities, roles, responsibilities, and the lasting impact leaders create.

1. Defining a Leader

A leader recognizes potential in people and situations and works intentionally to bring that potential to life. As established earlier in this book, leadership is the capacity to influence and inspire willing followership. Rather than redefining influence here, this chapter focuses on who carries influence and why people choose to follow certain individuals. True leaders are not followed because of position alone, but because of trust, credibility, and consistency of character.

1.1 Influence Over Authority

Authority may come with a title, but influence is earned.

True leaders inspire followership not because people must follow, but because they want to. Influence allows leaders to shape decisions, drive changes, and create lasting impact.

Position gives permission to speak.

Influence gives power to lead.

1.2 Visionary Thinking

Leaders think beyond the present. They see possibilities others overlook. Vision separates leaders from mere administrators.

A leader paints a compelling picture of the future and rallies people toward it with clarity and conviction.

2. The Qualities of a True Leader

Leadership is sustained by character. Without character, influence collapses.

2.1 Integrity

Integrity is the foundation of leadership. Leaders must be honest, ethical, and consistent. Integrity builds trust — and trust is the currency of leadership.

2.2 Empathy

Great leaders understand people. They listen, care, and respond with compassion. Empathy builds loyalty and belonging.

2.3 Resilience

Leaders face opposition, setbacks, and uncertainty. Resilience enables them to rise after failure and remain focused under pressure.

2.4 Decisiveness

Leaders make thoughtful but firm decisions. Indecision breeds confusion. Decisiveness builds momentum and confidence.

3. The Roles and Responsibilities of a Leader

A leader wears many hats in guiding people toward success.

3.1 The Visionary

Leaders define direction. They connect present action to future purpose and keep people aligned to mission.

3.2 The Coach

Leaders develop others. They give feedback, encouragement, and opportunity for growth.

3.3 The Facilitator

Leaders remove obstacles, resolve conflict, and create environments where teams perform at their best.

3.4 The Decision-Maker

While collaboration matters, leaders take responsibility for final decisions and outcomes.

4. The Impact of a Leader

Leadership impact is measured beyond results — it is seen in culture, people, and legacy.

4.1 Building Positive Culture

Leaders shape organizational atmosphere through behavior, expectations, and example.

4.2 Developing Future Leaders

Great leaders multiply leadership by mentoring and empowering others.

4.3 Driving Change and Innovation

Leaders challenge comfort zones, encourage creativity, and push progress forward.

5. Definitions and Perspectives on Leadership

Napoleon Bonaparte called a leader *"a dealer in hope."*

Benjamin Disraeli noted, *"I must follow the people. Am I not their leader?"*

Groucho Marx humorously observed, *"Only one man in a thousand is a leader — the rest follow."*

Dictionaries define a leader as one who goes before others to show the way. Together, these capture leadership as guidance, influence, and inspiration.

6. The Vision and Drive of a Leader

Leaders are dreamers with discipline. They see problems to solve and futures to build — and they pursue these relentlessly.

Vision without action is fantasy. Action without vision is chaos. Leaders combine both.

7. Traits and Expertise of Leaders

Key traits distinguish effective leaders:

- Integrity
- People skills
- Positivity
- Communication ability
- Strategic thinking

Leadership is both character and competence in action.

8. The Ultimate Outcome of Leadership

Leadership is not about title or popularity — it is about impact. Leaders inspire greatness in others, shape environments, and leave enduring influence.

9. Conclusion

A leader is one who inspires, guides, and empowers others toward shared purpose. Through integrity, empathy, resilience, and decisive action, leaders earn trust and multiply impact.

True leadership is measured not only by present achievements, but by the developed people and the legacy left behind.

This understanding completes the foundation of **The Core of Leadership** — preparing us to move deeper into leadership practice in the chapters ahead. Understanding who a leader is now prepares us to explore the key concepts that shape effective leadership.

KEY TAKEAWAYS

- Leadership is influence, not position.
- Integrity is the foundation of leadership
- Vision distinguishes leaders from managers
- Leaders develop people and culture
- Leadership impact is measured in legacy

REFLECTION QUESTIONS

1. Do people follow me by obligation or by inspiration?

2. How do I demonstrate integrity in daily leadership?

3. What vision am I currently casting to others?

4. Who am I intentionally developing as a future leader?

5. What legacy am I building through my leadership?

ACTION STEPS

1. Write your personal definition of a leader.

2. Ask someone why they choose to follow your leadership.

3. Strengthen one leadership quality this week.

4. Mentor or encourage one emerging leader.

5. Reflect weekly on leadership growth.

Closing Thought

A leader is not defined by title, but by responsibility, influence, and the courage to act.

CHAPTER 9 — What Every Leader Must Know

Introduction

Leadership is not accidental. It is learned, practiced, refined, and lived. Every effective leader must acquire certain principles, skills, and self-awareness to navigate complexity, inspire people, and drive meaningful results.

Leadership today demands more than authority — it requires vision, emotional intelligence, adaptability, ethics, and continuous growth. This chapter presents the essential knowledge, abilities, and attitudes every leader must develop to lead successfully in any environment.

1. Understanding Foundational Leadership Principles

1.1 Vision and Purpose

Every leader must carry a clear vision. Vision gives direction, meaning, and motivation — without it teams drift, but with it people unite toward shared purpose. Leaders must define, communicate, and embody the vision they expect others to follow.

1.2 Influence and Inspiration

Effective leadership relies on influence rather than force — leaders inspire people to contribute willingly through trust, credibility, and shared purpose.

1.3 Integrity and Ethics

Integrity is the cornerstone of sustainable leadership. Leaders must do what is right even when it is difficult. Ethical leadership builds trust — and trust builds long-term success.

1.4 Accountability and Responsibility

Leaders accept responsibility for outcomes. They own mistakes, celebrate team successes, and create cultures of accountability where excellence becomes normal.

2. Core Leadership Skills Every Leader Must Master

2.1 Communication

Leaders must communicate with clarity and purpose. They listen actively, speak meaningfully, and create understanding across all levels of the organization.

2.2 Decision-Making

Effective leaders make informed and timely decisions. They balance data, experience, and intuition while remaining courageous under uncertainty.

2.3 Problem-Solving

Leaders solve problems rather than avoid them. They analyze root causes, involve teams in solutions, and convert challenges into opportunities.

2.4 Emotional Intelligence

Great leaders understand themselves and others. Emotional intelligence allows leaders to manage pressure, navigate relationships, and lead with empathy and authenticity.

2.5 Delegation

Leaders multiply effectiveness by empowering others. Delegation develops people, increases ownership, and frees leaders to focus on strategic priorities.

3. Strategic Thinking and Planning

3.1 Goal Setting

Leaders set clear, measurable goals aligned with vision. Goals turn vision into actionable steps.

3.2 Long-Term Perspective

Leaders think beyond immediate demands. They anticipate trends, prepare for change, and guide organizations toward sustainable growth.

3.3 Risk Management

Wise leaders assess risks, prepare contingencies, and remain steady in uncertainty.

4. Team Leadership and Collaboration

4.1 Building Trust

Trust is the foundation of teamwork. Leaders build trust through consistency, transparency, and fairness.

4.2 Motivation and Empowerment

Leaders recognize effort, develop talent, and create environments where people flourish.

4.3 Conflict Resolution

Leaders address conflict constructively, restoring unity and focus.

4.4 Diversity and Inclusion

Leaders value differences, welcome perspectives, and build inclusive cultures that drive innovation.

5. Personal Leadership Growth

5.1 Continuous Learning

Leaders never stop growing. They read, reflect, seek mentorship, and learn from experience.

5.2 Self-Awareness

Leaders understand their strengths, blind spots, and impact on others.

5.3 Resilience and Adaptability

Leaders remain steady through pressure and flexible through change.

6. What Leaders Must Know About People

Leaders must understand the people they lead — their hopes, motivations, abilities, limitations, and aspirations. People follow leaders who genuinely care about them.

Leaders must facilitate meaningful communication, effective meetings, and shared experiences that strengthen unity.

They must also regularly evaluate team progress and personal leadership effectiveness.

7. Leadership in Action

Leaders turn clarity into action. They communicate honestly, build commitment, create learning cultures, remain persistent, and learn from experience.

Leadership is lived daily — not declared occasionally.

8. Conclusion

Leadership excellence is not mysterious. It is the result of understanding principles, mastering skills, developing character, and committing to continuous growth.

Every leader who embraces these essentials can inspire people, transform organizations, and leave enduring legacy.

That is what every leader must know. With these concepts in mind, we now move to explore the different levels at which leadership operates.

KEY TAKEAWAYS

- Vision gives direction

- Influence drives leadership

- Integrity sustains trust

- Communication builds alignment

- Emotional intelligence deepens connection

- Delegation multiplies capacity

- Strategic thinking secures future success

- Continuous growth sustains leadership excellence

REFLECTION QUESTIONS

1. Is my vision clear to those I lead?

2. How strong is my influence beyond my authority?

3. Do people trust my integrity?

4. How well do I handle difficult decisions?

5. What leadership skills must I strengthen next?

ACTION STEPS

1. Write your leadership vision in one paragraph.

2. Ask for feedback on your communication style.

3. Delegate one responsibility this week.

4. Read one leadership book this month.

5. Schedule weekly personal reflection time.

Closing Thought

Leadership is not about knowing everything; it is about knowing what matters most and acting on it.

CHAPTER 10 — The Levels of Leadership

Introduction

Leadership is not static. It grows, deepens, and expands through intentional development. Understanding the stages of leadership growth allows leaders to rise from authority to legacy.

One of the most practical frameworks for understanding leadership growth is John Maxwell's Five Levels of Leadership. These levels represent progression from authority-based leadership to legacy-based leadership.

This chapter explores each level, its defining characteristics, its challenges, and the opportunities it presents for leadership development.

1. The Five Levels of Leadership

Level 1: Position — Rights

At Level 1, leadership is based on title or formal authority. People follow because they must. Influence is limited to what the position grants.

Characteristics

- Reliance on formal authority
- Focus on rules, procedures, and structure
- Limited relational connection

Challenges

- Compliance without commitment
- Minimal influence beyond job description

Opportunities

- Learn leadership responsibilities

- Begin building credibility and trust

Position is the starting point — not the destination.

Level 2: Permission — Relationships

At Level 2, leadership is built on relationships. People follow because they want to. Trust, respect, and connection become the foundation of influence.

Characteristics

- People-first leadership

- Open communication

- Strong relational trust

Challenges

- Balancing relationships with performance

- Risk of avoiding difficult decisions to preserve harmony

Opportunities

- Build loyalty and engagement

- Creating positive team culture

Level 3: Production — Results

At Level 3, leadership is proven through results. People follow because the leader delivers success. Credibility grows through achievement.

Characteristics

- Results-oriented focus

- Clear goals and expectations
- High-performance culture

Challenges

- Risk of neglecting relationships
- Pressure to sustain performance

Opportunities

- Establish leadership credibility
- Inspire teams through achievement

Level 4: People Development — Reproduction

At Level 4, leadership shifts from producing results to producing leaders. People follow because the leader invests in their growth.

Characteristics

- Coaching and mentoring culture
- Empowerment of emerging leaders
- Multiplication of leadership capacity

Challenges

- Balancing short-term results with long-term development
- Managing resistance to growth

Opportunities

- Build leadership pipeline
- Create sustainable organizational success

Level 5: Pinnacle — Respect

At Level 5, leadership becomes legacy. People follow because of who the leader is and what they represent. Influence extends beyond organization and lifetime.

Characteristics

- Widely respected influence

- Wisdom, humility, integrity

- Broad societal or industry impact

Challenges

- Staying humble at high influence

- Using power responsibly

Opportunities

- Leave legacy

- Mentor leaders across generations

2. Moving Through the Levels

2.1 The Journey from Position to Pinnacle

Progression is intentional — not automatic. Leaders must grow in self-awareness, competence, and character at every stage.

2.2 The Role of Self-Leadership

Self-leadership remains the anchor of all levels. Those who cannot lead themselves cannot lead others effectively.

2.3 The Importance of Adaptability

Different situations require different leadership levels. Mature leaders adapt their style to meet people and circumstances effectively.

3. Challenges and Pitfalls at Each Level

Every level has blind spots. Authority dependence, relationship overemphasis, result obsession, or ego inflation can derail leadership growth. Awareness prevents stagnation.

4. Developing a Leadership Growth Plan

4.1 Assess Your Current Level

Regular reflection and feedback reveal where you truly operate — not just where you think you are.

4.2 Set Advancement Goals

Growth requires intentional learning, practice, and accountability.

4.3 Commit to Continuous Development

Leadership mastery is achieved through lifelong growth.

5. Leadership in Real Life

Whether a new manager earning trust, a results-driven executive driving performance, or a seasoned leader building successors — each level appears daily in real leadership journeys.

6. Conclusion: The Path to Leadership mastery

Leadership is a lifelong ascent. Each level expands influence, effectiveness, and impact. Mastery is not measured by how many people serve you — but by how many people you serve and develop.

Those who intentionally climb these levels not only achieve success — they leave legacy. Understanding the levels of leadership now brings us to a critical point of clarity — what leadership truly is and what it is not.

KEY TAKEAWAYS

- Leadership growth in levels
- Influence expands with trust and results
- Developing others multiplies leadership
- Legacy is the highest form of leadership
  - Growth through levels is intentional

REFLECTION QUESTIONS

1. Which level best describes my current leadership?
2. How am I building trust with my team?
3. Am I delivering consistent results?
4. Who am I actively developing?
5. What legacy am I building?

ACTION STEPS

1. Identify your current leadership level.
2. Ask for feedback from team members.
3. Invest in one person's growth this month.
4. Strengthen one leadership skill weekly.
5. Write a personal leadership legacy statement.

Closing Thought

Leadership grows through levels, but influence deepens with intentional growth and consistency.

CHAPTER 11 — What Leadership Is and Isn't

Introduction

Because leadership is so powerful, it is also widely misunderstood. Many confuse leadership with control, charisma, or popularity. Clarity is essential if leadership is to remain authentic.

To lead effectively, one must first understand the true nature of leadership. This chapter clarifies what leadership genuinely is — and what it is not — so readers can embrace authentic leadership grounded in purpose, service, and impact.

1. Define Leadership

Leadership expresses itself through influence, guidance, and inspiration — enabling people to move toward shared purpose with clarity and commitment. It is not dependent on title, rank, or authority, but on trust, credibility, and example.

True leadership aligns direction, people, and purpose — transforming intention into collective achievement.

2. What Is Leadership?

Leadership is Vision and Direction

Leaders see the future before others do. They set clear direction and align efforts toward meaningful goals.

Leadership is influence directed toward a shared purpose.

Leaders motivate others to follow willingly. They are inspired through words, actions, and consistency.

Leadership is Empowerment and Support

Leaders create environments where people feel valued, capable, and encouraged to grow.

Leadership is Collaboration and Teamwork

Leaders unite diverse strengths and perspectives to achieve outcomes no individual could accomplish alone.

Leadership is Integrity and Authenticity

Leaders act ethically, transparently, and consistently. Integrity builds trust — the foundation of lasting influence.

3. What Leadership Is Not?

Leadership is not Control or Domination

True leaders guide — they do not coerce. Leadership respects autonomy and dignity.

Leadership is not Micromanagement

Effective leaders trust people to perform. They provide guidance, not suffocation.

Leadership is not Ego or Self-Promotion

Leadership exists to elevate others, not glorify self.

Leadership is not Complacency

Leaders embrace innovation, improvement, and progress.

Leadership is not Indifference

Leaders care deeply about people and purpose. Apathy destroys leadership credibility.

4. The Essence of True Leadership

Authentic leadership is rooted in service, humility, responsibility, and empathy. Great leaders lead by example, cultivate trust, and empower others to become their best.

True leadership lifts people higher than they believed possible.

5. Conclusion

Leadership is neither title nor theatrics. It is vision, influence, integrity, and service in action. Understanding what leadership is — and what it is not — protects leaders from ego-driven distortion and grounds them in authentic purpose.

Those who lead with clarity, humility, and conviction become leaders worth following — and legacies worth remembering. With a clear understanding of what leadership is — and what it is not — we are now prepared to explore the essential qualities that define effective leaders.

KEY TAKEAWAYS

- Leadership is influence, not control.

- Leadership is service, not self-promotion

- Leadership is empowerment, not micromanagement

- Leadership is integrity, not manipulation

- Leadership is progress, not stagnation

REFLECTION QUESTIONS

1. Do I lead through influence or authority?

2. Do people feel empowered under my leadership?

3. How do I demonstrate integrity daily?

4. Where might ego be limiting my leadership?

5. How can I better serve those I lead?

ACTION STEPS

1. Write down what leadership means to you.

2. Identify one misconception you must unlearn.

3. Ask your team how they experience your leadership.

4. Practice empowerment by delegating meaningful responsibility.

5. Reflect weekly on servant leadership behaviors.

Closing Thought

Clarity defines leadership. When you understand what
leadership is—and what it is not—you lead with
confidence and direction.

CHAPTER 12 — Effective Leadership

Introduction

Knowing what leadership is prepares us for the next question: What makes leadership truly effective? The answer lies in character, competence, and consistent practice.

Effective leadership is the cornerstone of organizational success. It drives teams to achieve goals, inspires innovation, and sustains positive work environments. Leadership is not merely holding authority — it is the ability to guide people with vision, integrity, emotional intelligence, and adaptability.

Effective leaders create trust, develop people, navigate change, and deliver results while remaining grounded in purpose and values. This chapter explores the defining characteristics, skills, and practices that distinguish effective leaders in today's complex and dynamic world.

1. Core Characteristics of Effective Leaders

1.1 Visionary Thinking

Effective leaders see beyond the present. They anticipate opportunities, recognize threats, and chart strategic direction. Vision provides hope, clarity, and alignment.

As Napoleon Bonaparte said,"*A leader is a dealer in hope.*" Hope anchored in vision moves people forward.

1.2 Integrity and Ethics

As established earlier in this book, integrity is the foundation of leadership credibility and trust. In effective leadership, integrity moves beyond definition into daily practice — shaping decisions, relationships, and organizational culture. Ethical leaders act consistently, transparently, and responsibly, building trust that sustains long-term influence.

1.3 Emotional Intelligence

Leaders with emotional intelligence understand themselves and others. They manage emotions wisely, build strong relationships, resolve conflict constructively, and lead with empathy. Emotional intelligence transforms authority into connection.

1.4 Adaptability

Change is constant. Effective leaders remain flexible, open-minded, and ready to adjust strategies. Adaptable leaders learn quickly, embrace innovation, and guide teams confidently through uncertainty.

2. Essential Leadership Skills

2.1 Decision-Making

Leaders must make timely, informed, and courageous decisions. They balance data, experience, and intuition — then take responsibility for outcomes.

Peter Drucker captured it well: *"A leader is one who knows the way, goes the way, and shows the way."*

2.2 Communication

Leadership rises and falls on communication. Effective leaders listen actively, speak clearly, and ensure shared understanding. Communication builds trust, resolves conflict, and unites teams around vision.

2.3 Delegation

Delegation multiplies leadership capacity. Effective leaders assign responsibility based on strengths, provide guidance, and trust others to deliver. Delegation empowers growth and strengthens accountability.

2.4 Problem-Solving

Leaders confront challenges directly. They identify root causes, explore creative solutions, and turn problems into progress. Problem-solving keeps organizations resilient and forward moving.

3. Building High-Performing Teams

3.1 Fostering Positive Culture

Leaders shape culture through behavior and expectation. Positive cultures encourage trust, innovation, recognition, and shared ownership of success.

3.2 Empowering Team Members

Empowered people perform beyond expectation. Effective leaders provide resources, autonomy, and encouragement, creating confidence and accountability.

3.3 Encouraging Diversity and Inclusion

Diverse perspectives fuel creativity and innovation. Effective leaders welcome differences, create belonging, and harness collective intelligence.

3.4 Developing People Continuously

Great leaders invest in growth through mentoring, training, and opportunity. Development builds loyalty, competence, and leadership pipelines.

4. Navigating Change and Crisis

4.1 Leading Through Change

Effective leaders communicate clearly during transition, reduce uncertainty, and help teams understand purpose and direction. Change becomes opportunity under strong leadership.

4.2 Crisis Management

In crisis, leaders remain calm, decisive, and transparent. They protect people, stabilize systems, and sustain trust when it matters most.

4.3 Resilience and Persistence

Setbacks are inevitable. Effective leaders recover quickly, maintain optimism, and inspire perseverance in others.

5. The Continuous Journey of Leadership Growth

5.1 Self-Awareness and Reflection

Effective leaders examine their impact regularly. Reflection sharpens wisdom and authenticity.

5.2 Lifelong Learning

Leadership requires continuous learning. Great leaders remain students of growth, experience, and insight.

5.3 Mentorship and Coaching

Leaders grow through mentors and multiply influence by mentoring others. This ensures leadership continuity and legacy.

6. Conclusion

Effective leadership blends vision, integrity, emotional intelligence, competence, and resilience. It builds trust, develops people, and delivers results. Leadership is not an event — it is a lifelong practice of influence, service, and growth.

As Washington Irving said: *"Great minds have purposes; others have wishes."*

Effective leaders live by purpose — and turn purpose into impact. Understanding effective leadership now leads us to examine the most important questions that guide great leaders.

KEY TAKEAWAYS

- Vision provides direction
- Integrity builds trust
- Emotional intelligence builds connection
- Communication creates alignment
- Delegation multiplies capacity
- Adaptability sustains relevance
- Growth ensures lasting effectiveness

REFLECTION QUESTIONS

1. Is my vision clearly understood by my team?

2. Do people trust my integrity?

3. How well do I manage my emotions under pressure?

4. Am I empowering or controlling my team?

5. What leadership skills must I improve next?

ACTION STEPS

1. Write your leadership vision in one paragraph.

2. Ask a team member for honest feedback.

3. Delegate one meaningful responsibility this week.

4. Read one leadership article or chapter weekly.

5. Schedule monthly leadership self-reflection.

Closing Thought

Effective leadership is not accidental, it is the result of intentional action, discipline, and growth.

CHAPTER 13 — The Most Important Questions Effective Leaders Ask

Introduction

Effective leadership is not defined only by having the right answers — but by asking the right questions. Powerful questions unlock insight, challenge assumptions, inspire growth, and guide wise decision-making. The quality of a leader's questions often determines the quality of a team's thinking, performance, and progress.

Great leaders cultivate a culture of inquiry. They ask questions that clarify vision, strengthen alignment, expose blind spots, and stimulate continuous improvement. This chapter explores the most important questions effective leaders ask to guide their teams and organizations toward sustained success.

1. What Is Our Vision — and Does It Still Align with Our Values?

Vision gives direction. Values provide the compass. Leaders must regularly revisit both to ensure alignment between purpose and practice.

Key Insight: Clarity of vision and values keeps the organization united, focused, and inspired.

2. Are We Focusing on the Right Priorities?

Busyness is not productivity. Effective leaders constantly evaluate what truly matters and ensure energy is invested in high-impact activities.

Key Insight: Right priorities create meaningful progress.

3. How Can I Support You in Achieving Your Goals?

Leadership is service. This question opens dialogue, builds trust, and demonstrates genuine care for people's success.

Key Insight: Supportive leaders multiply confidence and commitment.

4. What Challenges Are You Facing — and How Can We Overcome Them Together?

Every team encounters obstacles. Leaders who ask this question identify problems early and encourage collaborative problem-solving.

Key Insight: Approachable leadership strengthens resilience.

5. What Might We Be Missing or Overlooking?

Blind spots limit progress. Wise leaders invite diverse perspectives and encourage critical thinking.

Key Insight: Great questions protect against costly oversight.

6. How Can We Improve Our Processes and Outcomes?

Continuous improvement keeps organizations relevant and competitive.

Key Insight: Progress begins with questioning the status quo.

7. What Are Our Customers or Stakeholders Saying About Us?

External feedback keeps leaders connected to reality. Listening to customers refines strategy and strengthens loyalty.

Key Insight: Customer insight guides sustainable excellence.

8. Are We Celebrating Our Successes Enough?

Recognition reinforces morale, motivation, and culture.

Key Insight: Celebrated success fuels future achievement.

9. What Are the Long-Term Implications of Today's Decisions?

Strategic leaders think beyond the moment.

Key Insight: Future-minded leadership prevents short-term mistakes.

10. Are We Living Up to Our Ethical Standards?

Integrity sustains trust. Leaders must regularly examine alignment between values and actions.

Key Insight: Ethical consistency preserves leadership credibility.

11. Who Else Should Be Involved in This Decision?

Inclusive leadership strengthens decisions and increases buy-in.

Key Insight: Shared wisdom leads to better outcomes.

12. Are We Leveraging People's Strengths Effectively?

Great leaders place people where they flourish.

Key Insight: Strength-based leadership multiplies performance.

13. What Have We Learned from Recent Successes or Failures?

Reflection turns experience into wisdom

KEY Insight: Learning cultures outpace stagnant ones.

14. How Do We Balance Innovation with Risk Management?

Progress requires creativity — stability requires wisdom. Effective leaders manage both.

Key Insight: Balanced leadership fuels sustainable innovation.

15. Are We Creating an Environment Where People Feel Valued and Heard?

Engaged people perform better and stay longer.

Key Insight: Belonging drives excellence.

The Power of Leadership Questions

The questions leaders ask shape the thinking of their teams. Wise questions create clarity. Courageous questions inspire change. Compassionate questions build trust.

The greatest leaders in history were not only great speakers — they were great questioners.

Conclusion

Leadership questions define leadership culture. When leaders ask thoughtful, strategic, and people-centered questions, they unlock insight, engagement, accountability, and progress.

Effective leaders understand this truth:

Answers give direction — but questions create transformation. These critical questions now prepare us to learn from great and effective leaders across different spheres of influence.

KEY TAKEAWAYS

- Great leaders ask great questions

- Questions clarify vision and values

- Questions uncover blind spots

- Questions build trust and engagement

- Questions drive continuous improvement

REFLECTION QUESTIONS

1. Do I ask more questions or give more instructions?

2. Which of these leadership questions do I ask regularly?

3. What question could transform my team right now?

4. Do people feel safe answering my questions honestly?

5. How can I improve my listening skills after asking questions?

ACTION STEPS

1. Choose three leadership questions to practice this week.

2. Ask one team member how you can better support them.

3. Add a reflection question to every team meeting.

4. Record insights gained from new questions.

5. Build a habit of weekly leadership inquiry.

Closing Thought

Great leaders ask the right questions — because the quality of your questions determines the quality of your leadership.

CHAPTER 14 — Great and Effective Leaders: Global Impact Across Spheres of Influence

Introduction

Leadership is a vital force that shapes societies, drives progress, and inspires transformation. Through history and continents, exceptional leaders have influenced politics, business, science, faith, education, culture, and community development. This Legacy Reference Edition presents 150 great and effective leaders whose lives demonstrate that leadership, when guided by vision, courage, integrity, and compassion, can change the course of history and uplift humanity.

Leadership Story

African Leadership Insight — Otumfuo Osei Tutu II

Otumfuo Osei Tutu II, the Asantehene of Ghana, represents a powerful model of leadership that blends tradition with transformation.

Under his leadership, the Ashanti Kingdom has not only preserved its rich cultural heritage but has also advanced in education, healthcare, and socio-economic development through strategic initiatives such as the Otumfuo Foundation.

His leadership demonstrates that tradition is not a limitation — it is a foundation for progress.

He has shown that a leader can:

- Honor the past

- Engage the present

- Build the future

This balance has made his leadership both respected and impactful on a global scale.

Leadership Insight

Great leaders do not choose between tradition and progress — they integrate both to create lasting impact.

Application

As a leader:

- Respect foundational values and culture

- Embrace innovation and change

- Build systems that create long-term transformation

Leadership becomes powerful when it connects legacy with vision.

SECTION 1 — POLITICAL AND GOVERNMENTAL LEADERS

(Legacy Reference Edition — Leaders 1–45)

1. POLITICAL AND GOVERNMENTAL LEADERS (1–15)

1. **Nelson Mandela (South Africa):** Led the fight against apartheid and became South Africa's first Black president, championing reconciliation and justice.

2. **Mahatma Gandhi (India):** Pioneer of nonviolent resistance whose leadership led India to independence and inspired global civil rights movements.

3. **Winston Churchill (United Kingdom):** Steadfast wartime leader who unified Britain during World War II and shaped modern democratic resilience.

4. **Kwame Nkrumah (Ghana):** Spearheaded Ghana's independence and championed Pan-Africanism, influencing Africa's decolonization.

5. **Franklin D. Roosevelt (United States):** Guided America through the Great Depression and World War II with transformative social and economic reforms.

6. **Angela Merkel (Germany):** Long-serving Chancellor who strengthened the European Union and led with pragmatic, steady leadership.

7. **Julius Nyerere (Tanzania):** Promoted African self-reliance and education, shaping Tanzania's post-independence identity.

8. **Lee Kuan Yew (Singapore):** Transformed Singapore into a global economic powerhouse through visionary governance.

9. **Abraham Lincoln (United States):** Preserved the Union and abolished slavery, redefining freedom and democracy.

10. **Haile Selassie (Ethiopia):** Modernized Ethiopia and became a symbol of African unity and resistance to colonialism.

11. **Margaret Thatcher (United Kingdom):** First female British Prime Minister who redefined economic policy and political leadership.

12. **Barack Obama (United States):** First African American U. S. President, inspiring global hope through inclusive leadership.

13. **Jacinda Ardern (New Zealand):** Recognized for compassionate and crisis-responsive leadership.

14. **Paul Kagame (Rwanda):** Led Rwanda's post-genocide transformation into a stable and economically growing nation.

15. **Thomas Sankara (Burkina Faso):** Revolutionary African leader who promoted integrity, self-sufficiency, and anti-corruption governance.
Leadership Lesson:
Courage + conviction + sacrifice = transformational leadership.

2. BUSINESS AND ECONOMIC LEADERS (16–30)

16. **Steve Jobs (United States):** Co-founded Apple Inc. , revolutionizing technology, design, and innovation culture.

17. **Elon Musk (United States):** Founder of Tesla and SpaceX, pushing boundaries in sustainable energy and space exploration.

18. **Mary Kay Ash (United States):** Empowered women globally through entrepreneurship and direct sales innovation.

19. **Bill Gates (United States):** Co-founded Microsoft and became a global philanthropic leader in health and education.

20. **Oprah Winfrey (United States):** Built a media empire and became a symbol of empowerment and influence.

21. **Warren Buffett (United States):** Legendary investor known for ethical wealth creation and philanthropy.

22. **Jeff Bezos (United States):** Founded Amazon, transforming global commerce and logistics.

23. **Aliko Dangote (Nigeria):** Africa's leading industrialist driving economic growth and manufacturing self-sufficiency.

24. **Jack Ma (China):** Founded Alibaba, revolutionizing digital commerce in Asia.

25. **Indra Nooyi (India/USA):** Former CEO of PepsiCo, championing corporate transformation and sustainability.

26. **Richard Branson (United Kingdom):** Founder of Virgin Group, known for bold entrepreneurial leadership.

27. **Carlos Slim (Mexico):** Telecommunications magnate who expanded connectivity across Latin America.

28. **Howard Schultz (United States):** Transformed Starbucks into a global brand through people-centered leadership.

29. **Ngozi Okonjo-Iweala (Nigeria):** Global economic reformer and Director-General of the WTO.

30. **Tony Elumelu (Nigeria):** Founder of AFRI capitalism, empowering African entrepreneurship.
Leadership Lesson:
Innovation + discipline + execution = sustainable success.

3. SCIENCE AND TECHNOLOGY LEADERS (31–45)

31. **Marie Curie (Poland/France):** Pioneer of radioactivity research and two-time Nobel Prize winner.

32. **Albert Einstein (Germany/USA):** Developed the theory of relativity, reshaping modern physics.

33. **Isaac Newton (United Kingdom):** Father of classical mechanics and universal gravitation.

34. **Thomas Edison (United States):** Inventor of the electric bulb and pioneer of industrial innovation.

35. **Grace Hopper (United States):** Computer programming pioneer and creator of the first compiler.

36. **Nikola Tesla (Serbia/USA):** Inventor whose work shaped modern electrical engineering.

37. **Alan Turing (United Kingdom):** Father of modern computing and artificial intelligence theory.

38. **Tim Berners-Lee (United Kingdom):** Inventor of the World Wide Web.

39. **Katherine Johnson (United States):** NASA mathematician whose calculations enabled space missions.

40. **Jane Goodall (United Kingdom):** Primatologist and conservation leader redefining wildlife research.

41. **Elon Musk (United States):** Visionary in futuristic transportation and space innovation

42. **Mark Zuckerberg (United States):** Founder of Facebook, reshaping global communication.

43. **Fei-Fei Li (China/USA):** AI research leader advancing ethical artificial intelligence.

44. **Dennis Ritchie (United States):** Creator of the C programming language.

45. **Ada Lovelace (United Kingdom):** Recognized as the world's first computer programmer.

Leadership Lesson:

Curiosity + persistence + vision = breakthrough impact.

SECTION 2 — RELIGIOUS AND SPIRITUAL LEADERS

(Legacy Reference Edition — Leaders 46–90)

4. RELIGIOUS AND SPIRITUAL LEADERS (46–60)

46. **Jesus Christ:** Founder of Christianity, whose teachings on love, forgiveness, and salvation have shaped billions of lives across generations.

47. **Muhammad (Peace Be Upon Him):** Founder of Islam, whose revelations and leadership established one of the world's major religions.

48. **The Dalai Lama (Tibet):** Global symbol of compassion, peace, and spiritual wisdom in Tibetan Buddhism.

49. **Pope Francis (Vatican City):** Leader of the Catholic Church, known for humility, social justice advocacy, and care for the poor.

50. **Mother Teresa (India):** Devoted her life to serving the sick and dying, embodying servant leadership through compassion.

51. **Martin Luther (Germany):** Sparked the Protestant Reformation, redefining religious freedom and faith practice.

52. **John Wesley (United Kingdom):** Founder of Methodism, promoting disciplined spiritual growth and social responsibility.

53. **Billy Graham (United States):** Evangelist who brought Christian teachings to global audiences through mass crusades.

54. **Archbishop Desmond Tutu (South Africa):** Spiritual and moral leader in the anti-apartheid movement and reconciliation process.

55. **Apostle Paul (Middle East/Europe):** Early Christian missionary whose teachings established foundational Christian doctrine.

56. **John Calvin (France/Switzerland):** Theologian who shaped Protestant theology and governance structures.

57. **Rick Warren (United States):** Global pastor and author of *The Purpose Driven Life*, inspiring purpose-based leadership.

58. **Ayatollah Khomeini (Iran):** Religious leader who led Iran's Islamic Revolution.

59. **Benedict XVI (Vatican City):** Former Pope recognized for theological scholarship and doctrinal leadership.

60. **T. D. Jakes (United States):** Modern faith leader influencing global audiences through leadership and empowerment teachings.

Leadership Lesson:
Faith + integrity + service = lasting influence.

5. EDUCATION AND ACADEMIC LEADERS (61–75)

61. **Maria Montessori (Italy):** Revolutionized education through child-centered learning methodology.

62. **Booker T. Washington (United States):** Founded Tuskegee Institute, expanding educational access for African Americans.

63. **John Dewey (United States):** Pioneer of progressive education and experiential learning philosophy.

64. **Malala Yousafzai (Pakistan):** Global advocate for girls' education and Nobel Peace Prize laureate.

65. **Nelson Mandela (South Africa):** Promoted education as a tool for liberation and empowerment.

66. **Paulo Freire (Brazil):** Author of *Pedagogy of the Oppressed*, transforming adult education globally.

67. **Horace Mann (United States):** Father of public education reform in America.

68. **Anita Borg (United States):** Advocate for women in computing and technology education.

69. **Kwame Nkrumah (Ghana):** Established educational institutions to build post-independence Africa.

70. **Sal Khan (United States):** Founder of Khan Academy, democratizing digital education worldwide.

71. **Rudolf Steiner (Austria):** Founder of Waldorf education system.

72. **Benjamin Bloom (United States):** Created Bloom's Taxonomy, shaping learning assessment globally.

73. **Wangari Maathai (Kenya):** Environmental educator linking sustainability with community empowerment.

74. **John Harvard (United States):** Benefactor whose legacy led to the founding of Harvard University.

75. **Sugata Mitra (India):** Innovator in self-directed learning through digital education experiments.
Leadership Lesson:
Knowledge + discipline + mentorship = generational impact.

6. COMMUNITY AND SOCIAL LEADERS (76–90)

76. **Martin Luther King Jr. (United States):** Led the Civil Rights Movement through nonviolent resistance.

77. **Cesar Chavez (United States):** Fought for migrant farmworkers' rights and dignity.

78. **Jane Addams (United States):** Social reformer who founded Hull House to support immigrants.

79. **Wangari Maathai (Kenya):** Founded the Green Belt Movement promoting environmental and women's rights.

80. **Desmond Tutu (South Africa):** Advocate for justice, reconciliation, and human dignity.

81. **Mother Teresa (India):** Global humanitarian serving the poorest of the poor.

82. **Rosa Parks (United States):** Catalyst of the Montgomery Bus Boycott and civil rights movement.

83. **Greta Thunberg (Sweden):** Youth leader in global climate justice activism.

84. **Kofi Annan (Ghana):** Former UN Secretary-General and peace advocate.

85. **Leymah Gbowee (Liberia):** Led women's peace movement ending Liberia's civil war.

86. **Fred Rogers (United States):** Children's television host promoting kindness and emotional intelligence.

87. **Helen Keller (United States):** Advocate for disability rights and empowerment.

88. **Harriet Tubman (United States):** Led enslaved people to freedom through the Underground Railroad.

89. **Ellen Johnson Sirleaf (Liberia):** Africa's first elected female president and social reformer.

90. **Jimmy Carter (United States):** Former U. S. president devoted to humanitarian and peace initiatives.
Leadership Lesson:
Compassion + service + commitment = lasting community impact.

SECTION 3 — ARTS, MUSIC, AND LITERARY LEADERS

(Legacy Reference Edition — Leaders 91–150)

This final part completes the **150 great and effective leaders** collection.

7. ARTS, MUSIC, AND LITERARY LEADERS (91–105)

91. **Leonardo da Vinci (Italy):** Renaissance polymath whose art and inventions reshaped human creativity.

92. **William Shakespeare (United Kingdom):** Greatest playwright whose works continue shaping global literature.

93. **Ludwig van Beethoven (Germany):** Revolutionary composer who transformed classical music.

94. **Maya Angelou (United States):** Poet and author whose writings inspire resilience and identity.

95. **Aretha Franklin (United States):** "Queen of Soul, "whose music empowered civil rights and women's movements.

96. **Pablo Picasso (Spain):** Artistic innovator who transformed modern visual art.

97. **Chinua Achebe (Nigeria):** Author of *Things Fall Apart*, redefining African literature globally.

98. **Toni Morrison (United States):** Nobel Prize-winning author exploring Black identity and history.

99. **Bob Marley (Jamaica):** Reggae icon promoting peace, unity, and social justice.

100. **Frida Kahlo (Mexico):** Artist whose work expressed resilience and cultural identity.

101. **Rabindranath Tagore (India):** Nobel laureate poet and philosopher shaping Asian literature.

102. **Langston Hughes (United States):** Voice of the Harlem Renaissance in literature and culture.

103. **Fela Kuti (Nigeria):** Afrobeat pioneer and political activist through music.

104. **J. K. Rowling (United Kingdom):** Author whose storytelling redefined modern literature.

105. **Banksy (United Kingdom):** Street artist influencing contemporary social commentary through art.

Leadership Lesson:

Creativity + expression + influence = cultural transformation

8. SPORTS AND ENTERTAINMENT LEADERS (106–120)

106. **Serena Williams (United States):** Tennis champion and advocate for gender equality.

107. **Muhammad Ali (United States):** Boxing legend and global symbol of courage and justice.

108. **Pelé (Brazil):** Football icon and ambassador of global sports unity.

109. **Jackie Robinson (United States):** Broke racial barriers in professional baseball.

110. **Michael Jordan (United States):** Basketball legend who redefined sports excellence.

111. **Lionel Messi (Argentina):** Football genius inspiring generations with skill and humility.

112. **Usain Bolt (Jamaica):** World's fastest man, symbol of athletic greatness.

113. **Simone Biles (United States):** Gymnast redefining excellence and mental health advocacy.

114. **LeBron James (United States):** Athlete, philanthropist, and community leader.

115. **Cristiano Ronaldo (Portugal):** Football superstar known for discipline and global influence.

116. **Tiger Woods (United States):** Golf legend overcoming adversity to redefine the sport.

117. **Oprah Winfrey (United States):** Media leader influencing global entertainment and empowerment.

118. **Dwayne "The Rock" Johnson (United States):** Entertainment icon and motivational leader.

119. **Beyoncé Knowles (United States):** Cultural icon empowering identity and excellence through music.

120. **Shakira (Colombia):** Global entertainer and humanitarian leader.

Leadership Lesson:

Talent + discipline + resilience = excellence under pressure.

9. KINGS, QUEENS, AND GLOBAL ROYAL LEADERS (121–135)

121. **Mansa Musa (Mali Empire):** Legendary ruler whose reign promoted trade, scholarship, and prosperity.

122. **Queen Elizabeth II (United Kingdom):** Longest-serving British monarch providing stability across generations.

123. **King Ashoka (India):** Emperor who promoted peace, tolerance, and Buddhism across Asia.

124. **Queen Nzinga (Angola):** Warrior queen who resisted colonial invasion with strategic brilliance.

125. **Shaka Zulu (South Africa):** Military innovator who unified the Zulu Kingdom.

126. **Cleopatra VII (Egypt):** Political strategist who influenced Roman Egyptian relations.

127. **King Louis XIV (France):** "Sun King" who centralized monarchy and cultural patronage.

128. **Emperor Meiji (Japan):** Modernized Japan into a global power.

129. **Queen Victoria (United Kingdom):** Oversaw the British Empire's global expansion.

130. **King Solomon (Israel):** Biblical monarch known for wisdom and governance.

131. **Queen Hatshepsut (Egypt):** One of Egypt's greatest female pharaohs.

132.   **King Tutankhamun (Egypt):** Symbol of Egypt's royal heritage.

133.   **Emperor Haile Selassie (Ethiopia):** Royal leader and African unity icon.

134.   **King Henry VIII (England):** Monarch who reshaped English religious structure.

135.   **Queen Ranavalona I (Madagascar):** Defender of Malagasy sovereignty.

Leadership Lesson:
Authority + stewardship + legacy = generational leadership impact.

10. AFRICAN KINGS, QUEENS, AND ROYAL FAMILY LEADERS (136–150)

136.   **Yaa Asantewaa (Asante Kingdom, Ghana):** Warrior queen who led resistance against British colonialism.

137.   **Otumfuo Osei Tutu II (Asante Kingdom, Ghana):**
The 16th Asantehene and custodian of the Golden Stool, Otumfuo Osei Tutu II has modernized traditional leadership by championing education, healthcare, cultural preservation, and socio-economic development through the Otumfuo Osei Tutu II Foundation, strengthening the relevance of African traditional governance in the modern era.

138.   **Queen Amina (Zazzau, Nigeria):**
Warrior queen who expanded her kingdom's territory through strategic military leadership.

139.   **King Sundiata Keita (Mali Empire):** Founder of the Mali Empire and architect of West African unity.

140.   **King Cetshwayo kaMpande (Zulu Kingdom, South Africa):** Led resistance against British colonial expansion.

141.   **King Prempeh I (Asante Kingdom, Ghana):** Defended Asante sovereignty during British invasion.

142.   **Kabaka Mutesa I (Buganda, Uganda):** Promoted diplomatic engagement and modernization.

143.   **Emperor Menelik II (Ethiopia):** Defeated Italian forces at Adwa, preserving African independence.

144.   **King Moshoeshoe I (Lesotho):** Founder of modern Lesotho through unifying leadership.

145.   **Queen Mother Idia (Benin Empire, Nigeria):** Influential royal strategist and protector of the kingdom.

146.   **King Lobengula (Ndebele Kingdom, Zimbabwe):** Resisted colonial encroachment in Southern Africa.

147.   **Ooni Adeyeye Enitan Ogunwusi (Ile-Ife, Nigeria):** Modern Yoruba royal leader promoting culture and youth empowerment.

148.   **Asantehene Opoku Ware II (Ghana):** Predecessor of Otumfuo Osei Tutu II, known for peacebuilding and diplomacy.

149.	**King Sobhuza II (Eswatini):** Longest-reigning monarch in African history, guiding national identity.

150.	**Queen Modjadji VI (Balobedu Kingdom, South Africa):** The Rain Queen, symbol of African heritage and matriarchal authority.

Leadership Lesson:

Heritage + wisdom + responsibility = generational leadership.

Learning from great leaders now leads us to identify the best leadership practices that can be applied in our own leadership journey.

KEY TAKEAWAYS

Great leadership transcends culture, geography, and era.

- Effective leaders influence society through vision, courage, and service.

- Leadership impact is measured by transformation, not position.

- Every generation produces leaders suited for its challenges.

- Studying great leaders provides models for personal leadership growth.

REFLECTION QUESTIONS

1. Which leader in this chapter inspires you most and why?

2. What leadership trait do you admire most in historical leaders?

3. How are you applying similar leadership qualities in your life?

4. What sphere of influence are you called to impact?

5. What legacy do you want future generations to remember you for?

ACTION STEPS

1. Select one leader from this chapter and study their life further this month.

2. Identify one leadership quality you will intentionally develop this week.

3. Write your personal leadership vision statement.

4. Find a mentor whose leadership reflects the values you admire.

5. Begin practicing leadership where you are, with what you have.

Closing Thought

Great leaders remind us that leadership is not reserved for the privileged few — it is accessible to all who accept responsibility, develop character, and commit to service. The stories in this chapter prove that one person, armed with conviction and vision, can reshape nations, industries, communities, and generations. May their examples ignite in you the courage to lead where you are called.

PART III — LEADERSHIP IN PRACTICE

A leader turns vision into action.

CHAPTER 15 — Best Leadership Practices

Introduction

Effective leadership is not just about possessing certain traits or qualities; it also involves adopting best practices that enhance a leader's ability to guide, inspire, and manage teams effectively. Successful leaders apply intentional practices that strengthen trust, improve performance, and sustain long-term organizational success. Below are proven leadership practices consistently demonstrated by effective leaders across industries and cultures.

1. Leading by Example

Practice:

Demonstrate the behavior you expect from others. Your actions should align with your words, showing commitment to the organization's values and goals.

Outcome:

Builds trust and credibility with your team, encouraging them to follow your lead.

2. Fostering Open Communication

Practice:

Encourage transparent, two-way communication. Make it

easy for team members to share ideas, feedback, and concerns.

Outcome:

Enhances collaboration, reduces misunderstandings, and fosters a culture of openness and innovation.

3. Empowering and Developing Others

Practice:

Invest in the growth and development of your team members by providing opportunities for learning, giving them challenging tasks, and mentoring them.

Outcome:

Leads to a more skilled, motivated, and confident team, capable of taking on greater responsibilities.

4. Visionary Thinking

Practice:

Clearly articulate a compelling vision for the future and outline the steps needed to achieve it. Ensure that the vision is shared and understood by all team members.

Outcome:

Aligns the team toward common goals and motivates them to work with purpose and dedication.

5. Decision-Making with Integrity

Practice:

Make decisions based on ethical considerations, fairness, and the well-being of all stakeholders. Be transparent about the decision-making process.

Outcome:

Earns respect and trust from the team and stakeholders, fostering a culture of ethical behavior.

6. Encouraging Innovation

Practice:

Create an environment where creativity is encouraged and new ideas are valued. Be open to change and willing to take calculated risks.

Outcome:

Drives continuous improvement and keeps the organization competitive and forward-thinking.

7. Building Strong Relationships

Practice:

Develop strong relationships with team members, peers, and stakeholders. Show empathy, respect, and appreciation for their contributions.

Outcome:

Strengthens teamwork, loyalty, and cooperation, leading to better overall performance.

8. Effective Delegation

Practice:

Delegate tasks and responsibilities appropriately, trusting your team to deliver results while providing them with the support they need.

Outcome:

Increases efficiency, allows leaders to focus on strategic issues, and helps team members grow in their roles.

9. Adaptability and Flexibility

Practice:

Be prepared to adapt your leadership style to suit changing circumstances and the diverse needs of your team. Stay flexible in your approach to problem-solving.

Outcome:

Enables the team to respond effectively to challenges and changes in the environment.

10. Accountability and Responsibility

Practice:

Hold yourself and your team accountable for actions and outcomes. Acknowledge mistakes and take responsibility for rectifying them.

Outcome:

Fosters a culture of accountability and ownership, leading to higher performance standards and continuous learning.

11. Recognizing and Rewarding Excellence

Practice:

Regularly recognize and reward the achievements and contributions of your team members. Tailor your recognition to be meaningful to the individual.

Outcome:

Boosts morale, motivates continued excellence, and reinforces positive behaviors.

12. Balancing Short-Term Wins with Long-Term Goals

Practice:

Focus on achieving short-term objectives while keeping the long-term vision in mind. Ensure that immediate actions are aligned with broader strategic goals.

Outcome:

Sustains momentum toward long-term success while achieving necessary milestones along the way.

13. Practicing Self-Reflection and Continuous Improvement

Practice:

Regularly reflect on your leadership practices and seek feedback. Be open to learning and adapting based on experiences and input from others.

Outcome:

Ensures ongoing personal growth and continuous improvement of leadership effectiveness.

14. Managing Conflict Constructively

Practice:

Address conflicts promptly and fairly, seeking solutions that respect all parties involved. Use conflict as an opportunity for growth and improvement.

Outcome:

Maintains a positive work environment and prevents conflicts from escalating or disrupting team cohesion.

15. Promoting a Positive Work Culture

Practice:

Foster a work environment that emphasizes respect, inclusion, and well-being. Encourage a healthy work-life balance and a supportive atmosphere.

Outcome:

Enhances employee satisfaction, reduces turnover, and improves overall organizational performance.

Conclusion

Implementing these best leadership practices significantly enhances a leader's effectiveness and the success of their team or organization. Leadership is an ongoing journey that requires continuous learning, adaptation, and commitment to building a positive and productive environment. By embracing these practices, leaders inspire excellence, cultivate trust, and drive sustainable success. With these best practices in mind, we now move to explore leadership philosophy and the beliefs that shape leadership behavior.

KEY TAKEAWAYS

The best leadership practices reveal timeless principles that separate average leaders from exceptional ones.

- Leadership is demonstrated more by actions than words.

- Trust is built through consistency and integrity.

- Empowered people produce exceptional results.

- Vision gives teams purpose and direction.

- Communication is the lifeblood of effective leadership.

- Innovation keeps organizations relevant.

- Accountability strengthens performance culture.

- Self-reflection keeps leaders growing.

REFLECTION QUESTIONS

Take a moment to reflect:

1. Which leadership practice do you naturally excel in?

2. Which practice do you need to strengthen most?

3. How well do your actions align with your leadership values?

4. Do your team members feel empowered or controlled?

5. How do you recognize excellence in others?

6. How do you respond when facing conflict or resistance?

7. What leadership habit will define your legacy?

Write your responses. Reflection transforms knowledge into mastery.

ACTION STEPS

Leadership grows through intentional practice.

1. Choose one leadership practice to improve this month.

2. Ask your team for honest feedback on your leadership.

3. Create a personal leadership development plan.

4. Schedule weekly self-reflection time.

5. Recognize one team member's contribution this week.

6. Delegate a responsibility that develops someone else.

7. Revisit your vision and align current actions with it.

Small actions, practiced consistently, build great leaders.

CLOSING THOUGHT

Great leadership is not accidental. It is practiced daily through intention, character, and service. The world does not lack followers — it waits for leaders who will rise.

CHAPTER 16 — Leadership Philosophy

Introduction

Leadership is not merely about holding a position of authority; it is a journey shaped by deeply held beliefs, values, and principles that guide every decision and action. A well-defined leadership philosophy forms the foundation of effective leadership, influencing how leaders interact with their teams, make decisions, and navigate challenges. This chapter explores the essence of leadership philosophy, its importance, key components, and the process of developing and living out a personal leadership philosophy.

What Is Leadership Philosophy?

A leadership philosophy is a set of guiding beliefs and principles that influence how a leader thinks, behaves, and leads. It acts as a personal blueprint, providing clarity and direction in decision-making, problem-solving, and relationship-building. Leadership philosophy is rooted in core values, shaped by personal experiences, and refined over time through reflection and learning. It evolves as leaders grow and encounter new challenges.

The following quotations capture profound truths about leadership thinking and belief formation:

1. "Small minds discuss people, average minds discuss events, great minds discuss ideas." — Anonymous

Interpretation:
Great leaders focus on ideas, vision, and innovation rather than gossip or trivial matters. They cultivate environments

where creative thinking, strategy, and possibility shape the future.

2. "Reality is what we take to be true…" — Gary Zukav

Interpretation:
A leader's perceptions shape beliefs, and beliefs shape reality. Effective leaders remain self-aware, challenge biases, and stay open to new perspectives, creating inclusive and forward-thinking organizations.

3. "The philosophy of the schoolroom in one generation will be the philosophy of government in the next." — Abraham Lincoln

Interpretation:
Leaders shape the future by the values they model today. Every leader is a custodian of tomorrow's culture.

The Importance of a Leadership Philosophy

1. Provides Clarity and Direction
A leadership philosophy serves as a compass for decisions and actions, especially during uncertainty.

2. Builds Consistency and Trust
When leaders consistently act according to clear principles, trust and stability grow.

3. Inspires and Motivates Others
Strong philosophies give teams purpose and shared identity.

4. Facilitates Self-Reflection and Growth
Leaders with defined philosophies continuously improve and adapt.

Core Components of a Leadership Philosophy

1. **Core Values** — Integrity, respect, accountability, compassion.

2. **Vision and Purpose — Alignment with Direction**
Rather than redefining vision, a leadership philosophy clarifies how a leader commits to pursuing, communicating, and staying faithful to an already established vision. Philosophy determines how vision is carried forward.

3. **Leadership Style** — Transformational, servant, adaptive, or situational.

4. **Beliefs About People** — Seeing potential in others.

5. **Decision-Making Approach** — Ethical, inclusive, and principled.

6. **Commitment to Development** — Continuous learning and mentorship.

Developing a Leadership Philosophy

1. **Self-Reflection**
Ask: What do I believe- How do I want to impact others-

2. **Learning from Experience** Successes and failures refine philosophy.

3. **Seeking Feedback**
Mentors and teams provide clarity.

4. **Articulating Philosophy:** Write it as a mission, manifesto, or guiding principles.

5. **Living the Philosophy**

Philosophy must be practiced, not merely stated.

Examples of Leadership Philosophies

- **Servant Leadership** — Serving others first.

- **Transformational Leadership** — Inspiring extraordinary performance.

- **Ethical Leadership** — Leading with integrity and fairness.

- **Adaptive Leadership** — Thriving through change.

My Personal Leadership Philosophy

1. Value People Above All

2. A Leader Is a Learner

3. Serve, Not to Be Served

4. Lead by Example

5. Leadership Can Be Learned

6. Leadership Is a Process

7. Lead Yourself Before Leading Others

8. Simplify Complexity

9. Proper Preparation Prevents Poor Performance

10. Obedience to Principles Builds Credibility

11. Understand Times and Seasons

12. Do Not Despise Small Beginnings

13. Unity Is Strength

14. Be Vigilant

15. Joy Is a Strength

16. Leaders Are Made, Not Born

17. Leaders Are Originals, Not Copies

18. Passion Rules

19. Trust Is the Foundation

20. Empowerment Comes from Within

21. Touch the Heart Before Engaging the Mind

22. Connecting Is a Leader's Responsibility

23. Involve the Whole Person

24. Lead People, Manage Things

25. Teach Others How to Treat You

26. Play to Strengths

27. Leadership Is a Choice

28. Leadership Is Influence, Not Position.

29. Win the Private Victory First

Key Set of Beliefs

- People are valuable and capable of growth.

- Life is a continuous learning journey.

- Effective organizations prioritize people and innovation.

- Leadership purpose is to serve, inspire, and guide.

- Vision and values drive sustainable success.

Conclusion

Leadership philosophy is the soul of leadership practice. It determines how a leader thinks, decides, responds, and inspires. My philosophy is grounded in service, growth, integrity, people development, and purpose. By living these principles daily, leaders create environments where people thrive, organizations flourish, and legacies endure. Understanding leadership philosophy now prepares us to explore leadership thinking and how leaders process ideas and decisions.

KEY TAKEAWAYS

- Leadership philosophy is the foundation of consistent leadership.

- Beliefs shape behavior, behavior shapes culture.

- Self-awareness strengthens leadership impact.

- Vision and values give direction.

- People-centered leadership produces lasting influence.

- Philosophy must be practiced, not just written.

- Legacy is built through daily principled action.

REFLECTION QUESTIONS

1. What values define my leadership?

2. How do my beliefs influence my leadership behavior?

3. What leadership philosophy best reflects my personality?

4. How do I want people to feel under my leadership?

5. What bias or mindset must I challenge?

6. How do I respond under pressure?

7. What legacy will my leadership leave behind?

Write your responses. Reflection transforms philosophy into purpose.

ACTION STEPS

1. Write your personal leadership philosophy statement.

2. Identify three values you will never compromise.

3. Ask a trusted colleague for leadership feedback.

4. Schedule monthly self-reflection time.

5. Mentor at least one person this quarter.

6. Model one leadership behavior you want your team to adopt.

7. Revisit your philosophy every year and refine it.

CLOSING THOUGHT

Leadership without philosophy is direction without a compass.

Leadership with philosophy becomes purpose with power.

Lead with clarity. Lead with conviction. Lead with legacy.

Champion Remain.

CHAPTER 17 — Leadership Thinking

Introduction

Leadership is not born first in action — it is born in thought. Every great leader in history distinguishes themselves not merely by what they did, but by how they thought. A leader's mind is the command center from which vision, decisions, courage, creativity, and resilience flow. Thought precedes action. Mind precedes movement.

As Scripture affirms: **"As a man thinketh in his heart, so is he." — Proverbs 23:7**

This chapter explores the power of leadership thinking, the mindset that separates leaders from followers, and how cultivating intentional thought patterns transforms leadership effectiveness and legacy.

Foundational Quotes on Leadership Thinking

- "If you think a thing is impossible, you'll make it impossible." — Unknown

- "You cannot always control circumstances, but you can control your own thoughts." — Charles Poppleton

- "As a man thinketh in his heart, so is he." — Proverbs 23:7 (KJV)

Mind is master power. It molds, shapes, and directs all action.

A leader's thoughts are seeds — and organizations are the harvest.

Watch Your Thoughts

"Watch your thoughts, for they become words; watch your words, for they become actions; watch your actions, for they become habits; watch your habits, for they become character; watch your character, for it becomes your destiny."

Leadership begins internally. If a leader allows fear, doubt, and limitation to dominate their thinking, those same limitations will govern their leadership. Conversely, when a leader cultivates faith, vision, courage, and possibility-thinking, those qualities spread throughout the team.

Organizations rarely rise above the thinking level of their leader.

Leaders Are Unique Thinkers

Leaders do not simply think more — they think differently.

Leaders Think Differently About Themselves

They see themselves as responsible for change, not victims of circumstance.

Leaders Think Differently About Others

They see potential where others see limitation.

Leaders Think Differently About Possibilities

They look for opportunities, not merely obstacles.

Leaders Think Differently About Life

They see challenges as classrooms, not prisons.

Your thinking → creates beliefs → shapes philosophy → influences attitude → guides perception → produces action.

It all begins in the mind.

How Successful Leaders Think

Effective leaders cultivate multiple dimensions of thinking:

1. Strategic Thinking

Seeing the big picture and planning forward.

2. Critical Thinking

Analyzing information objectively before deciding.

3. Creative Thinking

Generating new ideas and innovative solutions.

4. Systems Thinking

Understanding interconnections and ripple effects.

5. Reflective Thinking

Learning continuously from experience.

A leader who cannot think deeply cannot lead widely.

The Leadership Thinking Process

1. Recognize the issue

2. Define the problem clearly

3. Gather relevant information

4. Analyze patterns and implications

5. Generate solutions

6. Evaluate alternatives

7. Decide wisely

8. Implement intentionally

9. Reflect and learn

This disciplined thinking cycle distinguishes reactive managers from visionary leaders.

The Importance of Space and Place for Thinking

Great leaders schedule thinking time. They create thinking spaces.
They protect reflection moments.

Because clarity rarely appears in noise — it appears in stillness.

Leaders Think Big

Great leaders refuse small visions. They stretch imagination beyond current limitations.

"Dream no small dreams, for they have no power to move the hearts of men." — Goethe

Leaders Think of Others

Leadership thinking is never self-centered. It asks: "How will this decision impact my people-"

Leaders Think of Growth

They grow themselves so they can grow others. No leader ever outgrows their thinking capacity.

Conclusion

Leadership thinking is the birthplace of leadership impact.
Before you change systems, you must change thoughts.
Before you lead people, you must lead your mind.
Before you transform organizations, you must transform

perception. With the right mindset in place, we now examine the habits that sustain effective leadership.

As you think — so you become.

KEY TAKEAWAYS

- Leadership begins in the mind before it appears in action.

- Thoughts shape beliefs; beliefs shape leadership behavior.

- Leaders think differently about themselves, others, and possibilities.

- Strategic, critical, and creative thinking separates leaders from followers.

- Reflection refines leadership judgment.

- Thinking time is not a luxury, it is leadership necessity.

- A leader's thinking level sets the ceiling of organizational growth.

REFLECTION QUESTIONS

1. What dominant thoughts currently shape your leadership?

2. Do you think in terms of problems or possibilities?

3. How often do you intentionally create space for deep thinking?

4. Which type of thinking (strategic, creative, critical, reflective) do you need to strengthen most?

5. What belief about yourself might be limiting your leadership capacity?

6. If your team adopted your exact thinking patterns, what culture would emerge?

7. What new thought discipline will define your leadership legacy?

Write your answers. Reflection converts insight into wisdom.

ACTION STEPS

1. Schedule 30 minutes of uninterrupted thinking time weekly.

2. Identify one limiting belief and replace it with an empowering belief.

3. Practice asking "What's possible-" before "What's wrong-"

4. Keep a leadership thinking journal for insights and reflections.

5. Before major decisions, pause and apply the full thinking process.

6. Expose yourself to new ideas through reading and learning.

7. Teach your team to think — not merely to follow instructions.

Small disciplines in thinking produce great leadership outcomes.

CLOSING THOUGHT

The greatest battlefield of leadership is not the boardroom
—

it is the mind.

Win the battle of thinking, and you win the future of
leadership.

Champion Remain.

CHAPTER 18 — The Habits of Effective Leaders

Introduction

Leadership is not merely about making decisions or guiding teams; it is about cultivating habits that consistently drive success. Effective leaders are distinguished not only by their skills and knowledge, but by the daily practices they repeat until excellence becomes natural. Habits form the backbone of leadership character. They shape how leaders think, act, respond, and influence others. This chapter explores the essential habits of effective leaders and how these habits sustain long-term leadership excellence.

The Importance of Habits in Leadership

Habits are repeated behaviors that become second nature, shaping consistency, credibility, and performance over time. For effective leaders, strong habits are essential because they:

- Ensure consistency between values and actions

- Enhance productivity and focus

- Build trust and reliability

- Foster continuous growth

- Sustain long-term effectiveness

Leadership greatness is rarely accidental — it is habitual.

Key Habits of Effective Leaders

Habit 1: Being Proactive

Effective leaders take initiative. They create opportunities rather than wait for them. Proactive leaders focus on what they can control and influence.

How to Develop This Habit:

- Set clear goals and take the first step
- Focus on solutions, not problems
- Practice making timely decisions

Habit 2: Beginning with the End in Mind

Leaders operate with vision. They define destination before beginning the journey.

How to Develop This Habit:

- Write personal and organizational mission statements
- Visualize desired outcomes
- Plan backward from vision to action

Habit 3: Prioritizing and Managing Time

Effective leaders focus on what matters most, not merely what is urgent.

How to Develop This Habit:

- Use priority tools (Eisenhower Matrix)
- Protect focused work time
- Delegate appropriately

Habit 4: Embracing a Growth Mindset

Leaders are lifelong learners. They grow through feedback, challenges, and continuous improvement.

How to Develop This Habit:

- Seek feedback regularly
- Embrace challenges
- Invest in learning

Habit 5: Practicing Empathy

Leaders listen deeply and value people genuinely. Empathy builds trust and loyalty.

How to Develop This Habit:

- Practice active listening
- Consider others before decisions
- Show genuine care

Habit 6: Building Strong Relationships

Leadership is relational. Influence grows where trust is nurtured.

How to Develop This Habit:

- Invest time in people
- Encourage collaboration
- Communicate consistently

Habit 7: Maintaining a Balanced Life

Effective leaders protect physical, emotional, and spiritual well-being.

How to Develop This Habit:

- Set healthy boundaries

- Practice self-care

- Make time for renewal

Habit 8: Practicing Accountability

Great leaders take responsibility and foster responsibility in others.

How to Develop This Habit:

- Set clear expectations

- Follow through on commitments

- Address mistakes honestly

Habit 9: Communicating Clearly and Effectively

Leadership rises or falls on communication.

How to Develop This Habit:

- Speak with clarity

- Listen before responding

- Keep people informed

Habit 10: Reflecting and Learning from Experience

Reflection transforms experience into wisdom.

How to Develop This Habit:

- Schedule reflection time

- Journal lessons learned

- Adjust based on insight

Covey's Seven Habits — A Leadership Perspective

Stephen Covey's framework remains foundational:

- Be Proactive

- Begin with the End in Mind

- Put First Things First

- Think Win-Win

- Seek First to Understand, Then to Be Understood

- Synergize

- Sharpen the Saw

These habits form a timeless leadership blueprint.

Conclusion

The habits of effective leaders are not occasional behaviors — they are disciplined daily practices. Leadership is not defined by what you do once, but by what you do consistently. When strong habits become embedded in character, leadership excellence follows naturally. These habits now lead us to explore the guiding principles that shape consistent leadership behavior.

KEY TAKEAWAYS

- Leadership excellence is built through daily habits.

- Consistency builds credibility.

- Vision directs habits toward purpose.

- Growth mindset sustains adaptability.

- Empathy strengthens influence.

- Accountability builds trust.

- Reflection turns experience into wisdom.

REFLECTION QUESTIONS

1. Which leadership habit is currently your strongest?

2. Which habit needs the most improvement?

3. Do your daily routines align with your leadership vision?

4. How well do you practice empathy with your team?

5. What habit will most shape your leadership legacy?

Write your responses. Reflection transforms awareness into mastery.

ACTION STEPS

1. Select one leadership habit to strengthen this month.

2. Ask someone for honest feedback on your leadership habits.

3. Design a daily leadership routine.

4. Schedule weekly reflection time.

5. Practice proactive decision-making this week.

6. Recognize one person's contribution today.

7. Protect time for learning and renewal.

Small consistent actions create extraordinary leaders.

CLOSING THOUGHT

Leadership is not a single act. It is the sum of daily choices repeated with purpose. Build the right habits — and your legacy will build itself.

Champion Remain.

CHAPTER 19 — Leadership Principles

"If your actions inspire others to dream more, learn more, do more, and become more, you are a leader." — **John Quincy Adams**

Introduction

Effective leadership transcends mere authority — it is the embodiment of timeless principles that guide decisions, actions, and relationships. While methods may change with circumstances, principles remain constant. They form the moral and strategic compass that distinguishes great leaders from average ones. Leaders who live by sound principles inspire trust, foster collaboration, and drive sustainable progress.

As John C. Maxwell states:

"A leader is one who knows the way, goes the way, and shows the way."

This chapter explores the foundational principles every leader must embrace to build credibility, influence, and enduring impact.

What Is a principle-

A principle is a fundamental law, truth, or moral guideline that directs behavior. Unlike techniques which may evolve, principles are enduring. They govern consistency, character, and credibility in leadership.

CORE PRINCIPLES OF EFFECTIVE LEADERSHIP

1. Integrity

Definition: Doing what is right, even when no one is watching.
Importance: Integrity is the foundation of trust.
Application: Align words with actions. Uphold ethical standards.

2. Vision

Definition: Seeing beyond the present to a greater future.
Importance: Vision provides direction and motivation.
Application: Communicate vision clearly and passionately.

3. Empathy

Definition: Understanding and valuing others' feelings.
Importance: Builds strong relationships and trust.
Application: Practice active listening and compassion.

4. Accountability

Definition: Taking responsibility for actions and outcomes.
Importance: Creates performance culture and reliability.
Application: Model responsibility and expect it from others.

5. Adaptability

Definition: Embracing change with flexibility.

Importance: Keeps leadership relevant in dynamic environments. **Application:** Remain open to new ideas and innovation.

6. Courage

Definition: Standing for truth and making difficult decisions.
Importance: Inspires confidence and bold progress.
Application: Act decisively despite fear or opposition.

7. Humility

Definition: Serving rather than seeking personal glory.
Importance: Makes leaders approachable and teachable.
Application: Celebrate others' success and accept feedback.

8. Transparency

Definition: Open and honest communication.
Importance: Reduces uncertainty and builds trust.
Application: Share information clearly and consistently.

9. Decisiveness

Definition: Ability to make timely, confident decisions.
Importance: Provides clarity and direction.
Application: Gather facts, decide, and communicate promptly.

10. Servant Leadership

Definition: Prioritizing the needs of others.
Importance: Builds empowered and loyal teams.
Application: Remove obstacles and equip people to succeed.

11. Commitment to Continuous Improvement

Definition: Pursuing ongoing growth personally and organizationally.
Importance: Sustains excellence and innovation.
Application: Encourage learning and feedback culture.

12. Focus on Results

Definition: Driving measurable outcomes.

Importance: Ensures effective use of time and resources.

Application: Set clear objectives and track progress.

ADDITIONAL LEADERSHIP PRINCIPLES

13. Empowerment — Giving people authority to own their work.

14. Collaboration — Harnessing collective strength.

15. Cultural Awareness — Valuing diversity and inclusion.

16. Emotional Intelligence — Managing self and relationships wisely.

17. Innovation — Encouraging creativity and experimentation.

18. Resilience — Rising through adversity.

19. Fairness & Justice — Acting without bias or favoritism.

20. Humor & Positivity — Sustaining morale and energy.

21. Stewardship — Managing resources responsibly.

22. Clarity — Communicating expectations plainly.

23. Discipline — Maintaining consistency and follow-through.

24. Gratitude — Recognizing contributions and success.

THE BE – KNOW – DO LEADERSHIP FRAMEWORK

BE

Character, integrity, humility, authenticity.

KNOW

Knowledge, competence, continuous learning.

DO

Action, accountability, execution, results.

Great leadership balances all three.

TEN PRACTICAL PRINCIPLES OF LEADERSHIP

1. Know yourself and pursue self-development.

2. Be competent in your role.

3. Seek responsibility and accept accountability.

4. Make sound and timely decisions.

5. Lead by example.

6. Know your people and care for their well-being.

7. Keep people informed.

8. Build ownership and responsibility in others.

9. Ensure tasks are understood and achieved.

10. Equip people to function as a team.

DR. MYLES MUNROE'S SEVEN PRINCIPLES OF EAGLES

1. Eagles fly alone at high altitude — true leaders rise above crowds.

2. Eagles have strong vision — leaders stay focused on purpose.

3. Eagles do not eat dead things — leaders stay current and relevant.

4. Eagles love storms — leaders grow through challenges.

5. Eagles test before they trust — leaders build reliable partnerships.

6. Eagles prepare their nests — leaders develop their people.

7. Eagles renew themselves — leaders practice reflection and restoration.

CONCLUSION

The principles of leadership form the invisible architecture behind great influence. When leaders live by integrity, vision, empathy, accountability, courage, and service, they create organizations that thrive and legacies that endure. Leadership is not merely achieving results — it is shaping people, culture, and destiny.

Great leaders soar like eagles — rising above challenges, staying focused on vision, and inspiring others to fly higher. Understanding these principles now prepares us to examine the functions that leaders perform in practice.

KEY TAKEAWAYS

- Principles are permanent; methods change.

- Integrity is the foundation of leadership trust.

- Vision gives leadership direction.

- Empathy strengthens influence.

- Accountability builds performance culture.

- Courage moves leadership forward.

- Humility keeps leaders grounded.

- Continuous improvement sustains excellence.

- Empowerment multiplies leadership impact.

- Legacy is built through principled living.

REFLECTION QUESTIONS

1. Which leadership principle defines you most?

2. Which principle do you need to strengthen?

3. Do your actions align with your stated values?

4. How do you demonstrate integrity under pressure?

5. How clearly do you communicate vision?

6. Are you empowering or controlling others?

7. How do you respond to change and adversity?

8. What principle will define your leadership legacy?

Write your answers — reflection converts knowledge into
wisdom.

ACTION STEPS

1. Identify your top three leadership principles.

2. Write a personal leadership code of conduct.

3. Ask your team which principle they most see in
you.

4. Strengthen one weak principle this month.

5. Practice servant leadership in one tangible way
this week.

6. Make one courageous decision you've been
delaying.

7. Celebrate someone else's success publicly.

Small principled actions build great leadership
legacies.

CLOSING THOUGHT

Leadership without principles is influence without direction.
Leadership with principles becomes legacy without
expiration.

Champion Remain.

CHAPTER 20 — Leadership Functions

"The task of the leader is to get their people from where they are to where they have not been." — **Henry Kissinger**

Introduction

Leadership is not merely holding a position of authority — it is fulfilling essential responsibilities that guide, influence, and support people toward a shared goal. The effectiveness of any organization rises or falls on how well its leaders perform their functions and duties. These responsibilities establish direction, culture, discipline, motivation, and momentum.

Great leaders do not only manage tasks — they mobilize people, shape environments, and build pathways to purpose. This chapter explores the core functions and duties that define effective leadership in practice.

THE PRIMARY FUNCTIONS OF A LEADER

1. Vision Setting

Defining the Vision

A leader establishes a clear and compelling picture of the future. Vision acts as a roadmap guiding decisions and actions.

Communicating Vision

Leaders ensure that everyone understands the vision and sees their role in achieving it.

Inspiring Commitment

Beyond explanation, leaders ignite belief in the vision.

"You can't blow an uncertain trumpet." — Theodore M. Hesburgh

2. Strategic Planning

Developing Strategy

Leaders analyze internal and external realities to chart the course forward.

Resource Allocation

They assign people, finances, and tools efficiently to accomplish goals.

Setting Milestones

Leaders define measurable goals to maintain progress.

"Strategy is not the consequence of planning, but its starting point." — Henry Mintzberg

3. Decision-Making

Assessing Information

Leaders gather insight, evaluate risks, and consider perspectives.

Making Timely Decisions

Effective leaders avoid paralysis and act decisively.

Taking Responsibility

Leaders own the outcome of every decision.

"It is our choices that show what we truly are." — J. K. Rowling

4. Team Building and Development

Recruiting the Right People

Leaders build teams aligned with values and mission.

Developing Talent

They mentor, train, and create growth opportunities.

Fostering Collaboration

Leaders create unity, trust, and shared purpose.

"A leader's role is to guide, energize, and excite." — Jack Welch

5. Motivation and Inspiration

Encouraging Engagement

Leaders create environments where people feel meaningful.

Recognizing Effort

They celebrate achievement and reinforce excellence.

Leading by Example

Leaders model the behavior they expect.

"The function of leadership is to produce more leaders, not more followers." — Ralph Nader

6. Communication

Active Listening

Leaders listen to understand, not merely to respond.

Clear Messaging

They communicate consistently and transparently.

Constructive Feedback

Leaders build performance through dialogue.

"The art of communication is the language of leadership." — James Humes

7. Problem-Solving and Conflict Resolution

Identifying Problems Early

Leaders detect challenges before escalation.

Developing Solutions

They engage teams in creative problem-solving.

Resolving Conflict

Leaders mediate fairly and restore harmony.

"Leadership is solving problems." — Colin Powell

8. Change Management

Leading Change

Leaders introduce transformation with clarity.

Reducing Resistance

They address fear through involvement and support.

Sustaining Change

Leaders embed change into culture.

"Change is the law of life." — John F. Kennedy

9. Ethical Leadership

Modeling Integrity

Leaders demonstrate ethical behavior.

Ensuring Accountability

They uphold standards consistently.

Promoting Fairness

Leaders treat people with equity and respect.

"Ethics is knowing what is right to do." — Potter Stewart

10. Performance Management

Setting Expectations

Leaders define clear performance standards.

Monitoring Progress

They track goals and provide guidance.

Providing Support

Leaders equip people to succeed.

"Leadership is taking care of those in your charge." — Simon Sinek

AUTHORITY, RESPONSIBILITY, AND ACCOUNTABILITY

Authority

The right to direct and make decisions.

Responsibility

The duty to fulfill leadership obligations.

Accountability

Owning results — success or failure.

These three pillars sustain credible leadership.

FIVE ESSENTIAL INGREDIENTS OF EFFECTIVE LEADERSHIP

1. **Trust** — Built through consistency and integrity.

2. **Service** — Leadership exists to serve people.

3. **Action** — Leaders move vision into reality.

4. **Vision** — Leaders know where they are going.

5. **Team Competence** — Leaders build capable people.

"Leadership is about one life influencing another."
— John C. Maxwell

THE 2 R's OF TRUE LEADERSHIP

Results — Achieving meaningful outcomes.

Relationships — Building people while building performance.

True leadership balances both.

THE BE – KNOW – DO MODEL

BE — Character and values. **KNOW** — Understanding self, people, and mission. **DO** — Acting to achieve results.

"Leadership is the capacity to translate vision into reality."
— Warren Bennis

WHAT EVERY LEADER NEEDS TO FUNCTION EFFECTIVELY

Wisdom • Knowledge • Understanding • Vision • Mission • Humility • Courage • Character • Charisma • Confidence

These traits equip leaders to fulfill their duties with excellence.

CONCLUSION

The functions and duties of leadership are the daily expressions of vision, character, and service. When leaders set direction, make sound decisions, develop people, manage change, solve problems, and uphold ethics — organizations thrive.

Leadership is not about controlling people but guiding them toward their highest potential. With these functions in mind, we now turn to the qualities that define an effective leader.

KEY TAKEAWAYS

- Leadership functions create organizational direction.

- Vision precedes effective leadership action.

- Decision-making defines leadership courage.

- Team development multiplies leadership impact.

- Communication sustains trust.

- Ethical leadership builds credibility.

- Change management secures the future.

- Results and relationships measure leadership success.

REFLECTION QUESTIONS

1. Which leadership function do you perform best?

2. Which function needs strengthening?

3. How clearly do you communicate vision?

4. How do you handle decision pressure?

5. Do your team members feel supported?

6. How do you address conflict?

7. What leadership duty will define your legacy?

Write your reflections.

Reflection transforms duty into mastery.

ACTION STEPS

1. Write a clear statement for your team.

2. Schedule monthly team development sessions.

3. Improve your listening in every meeting this week.

4. Delegate one responsibility to develop someone.

5. Make one courageous decision you've delayed.

6. Recognize a team member publicly.

7. Review your leadership duties weekly.

Small daily duties produce great legacies.

CLOSING THOUGHT

Leadership is not measured by position. It is measured by fulfilling responsibility.

Champion Remain.

CHAPTER 21 — Qualities of an Effective Leader

"If your actions inspire others to dream more, learn more, do more, and become more — you are a leader." — **John Quincy Adams**

Introduction

Effective leadership is not defined by title or position but by character and conduct. The ability to inspire, guide, and influence others comes from inner qualities that shape outward behavior. Great leaders stand out because of who they are, not merely what they do.

These leadership qualities form the foundation of trust, credibility, influence, and long-term impact. In this chapter, we explore the essential qualities that define truly effective leaders.

CORE QUALITIES OF EFFECTIVE LEADERS

1. Visionary Thinking

Definition:
The ability to see beyond the present and define a compelling future.

Importance:
Vision gives purpose, direction, and motivation. Without vision, people wander. With vision, they move forward with passion.

Expression:
Visionary leaders clearly articulate where they are going and inspire others to follow.

2. Integrity

Definition:

Consistency between words, values, and actions.

Importance:

Integrity builds trust. Without trust, leadership collapses.

Expression:

Leaders with integrity do the right thing — even when no one is watching.

3. Emotional Intelligence

Definition:

The ability to understand and manage emotions — both personal and relational.

Importance:

High EQ strengthens communication, conflict resolution, and team harmony.

Expression:

Emotionally intelligent leaders connect deeply with people.

4. Adaptability

Definition:

The ability to adjust quickly to change.

Importance:

In a fast-changing world, adaptable leaders remain relevant and effective.

Expression:

They embrace change rather than resist it.

5. Decisiveness

Definition:

The ability to make clear and timely decisions.

Importance:

Indecision creates confusion. Decisiveness creates momentum.

Expression:

Decisive leaders act confidently and accept responsibility for outcomes.

6. Communication Skill

Definition:

The ability to express ideas clearly and listen actively.

Importance:

Communication is the bloodstream of leadership.

Expression:

Effective leaders speak with clarity and listen with intention.

7. Accountability

Definition:

Owning responsibility for actions and results.

Importance:

Accountable leaders build cultures of responsibility and excellence.

Expression:

They never blame — they learn and improve.

8. Empathy

Definition:

Understanding and valuing the feelings of others.

Importance:

Empathy builds loyalty, trust, and psychological safety.

Expression:

Empathetic leaders lead hearts, not just hands.

9. Confidence

Definition:

Belief in one's ability to lead effectively.

Importance:

Confidence inspires confidence in others.

Expression:

Confident leaders remain calm under pressure.

10. Humility

Definition:

Recognizing leadership is service, not superiority.

Importance:

Humility keeps leaders teachable and approachable.

Expression:

Humble leaders lift others instead of elevating themselves.

GREAT LEADERS IN ACTION — QUALITIES EXEMPLIFIED

- **Nelson Mandela** — Vision, forgiveness, integrity

- **Martin Luther King Jr.** — Inspiration, courage, moral conviction

- **Mother Teresa** — Compassion, humility, service

- **Winston Churchill** — Courage, resilience, decisiveness

- **Steve Jobs** — Vision, innovation, adaptability

- **Jacinda Ardern** — Empathy, emotional intelligence

- **John C. Maxwell** — Mentorship, communication, empowerment

These leaders influenced generations because their qualities outlived their positions.

CONCLUSION

Effective leadership is an inside-out journey. Skills can be learned — but qualities must be cultivated. Vision without integrity fails. Confidence without humility collapses. Communication without empathy disconnects.

When leaders develop these qualities, they create environments where people grow, organizations thrive, and legacies endure.

Leadership is not about being followed.

It is about being worth following. Having explored these qualities, we now move to examine the essential skills and abilities required for leadership.

KEY TAKEAWAYS

- Leadership flows from character before competence

- Vision gives direction

- Integrity builds trust

- Emotional intelligence strengthens relationships

- Adaptability sustains relevance

- Communication creates alignment

- Accountability produces excellence

- Humility preserves growth

REFLECTION QUESTIONS

1. Which leadership quality is your strongest?

2. Which quality needs deliberate development?

3. Do people experience you as approachable?

4. How well do you handle emotional pressure?

5. Are you known more for vision or integrity?

6. How do you respond to mistakes?

7. What qualities will define your leadership legacy?

Write your answers. Self-awareness unlocks transformation.

ACTION STEPS

1. Identify one leadership quality to develop this month.

2. Ask someone you trust for honest feedback.

3. Practice active listening daily this week.

4. Make one courageous decision you've delayed.

5. Recognize someone's contribution publicly.

6. Read one leadership book on character development.

7. Reflect weekly on your leadership growth.

Small character investments build great leaders.

CLOSING THOUGHT

Titles make managers. Qualities make leaders. Legacy makes the difference.

Champion Remain.

CHAPTER 22 — Leadership Skills and Abilities

"Leadership is the capacity to translate vision into reality."
— **Warren Bennis**

Introduction

Leadership is more than holding authority — it is mastering the skills and abilities that move people toward purpose. Effective leaders combine knowledge, competence, and emotional mastery to inspire teams, solve problems, and drive sustainable progress.

In today's complex and fast-changing world, leadership effectiveness depends not only on character but on developed abilities. This chapter explores the essential leadership skills every leader must cultivate to remain relevant, effective, and impactful.

THE IMPORTANCE OF LEADERSHIP SKILLS

Leadership skills empower leaders to:

- Inspire and motivate people toward excellence
- Make sound and timely decisions
- Communicate vision with clarity
- Solve problems strategically
- Build trust-based relationships
- Lead confidently through uncertainty

Skills turn potential into performance. Abilities turn vision into results.

ESSENTIAL LEADERSHIP SKILLS AND ABILITIES

1. Communication mastery

Essence:

The ability to express ideas clearly and listen intentionally.

Impact:

Clear communication aligns teams and prevents confusion.

Expression:

Great leaders speak with clarity and listen with empathy.

2. Emotional Intelligence (EQ)

Essence:

Understanding and managing emotions — yours and others.

Impact:

High EQ strengthens relationships and team harmony.

Expression:

Emotionally intelligent leaders lead people, not just processes.

3. Decision-Making Ability

Essence:

Analyzing information and choosing wisely under pressure.

Impact:

Decisive leaders keep organizations moving forward.

Expression:

They weigh options, act promptly, and own outcomes.

4. Strategic Thinking

Essence:

Seeing the big picture and planning long-term directions.

Impact:

Strategic leaders anticipate trends and prepare ahead.

Expression:

They lead today with tomorrow in mind.

5. Problem-Solving Skill

Essence:

Identifying root causes and developing effective solutions.

Impact:

Problem-solvers turn challenges into opportunities.

Expression:

They think critically, creatively, and calmly.

6. Conflict Resolution

Essence:

Managing disagreements fairly and constructively.

Impact:

Healthy conflict handling builds stronger teams.

Expression:

Leaders listen first, mediate wisely, and restore unity.

7. Team Building Ability

Essence:

Developing people and fostering collaboration.

Impact:

Strong teams multiply leadership effectiveness.

Expression:

Leader's mentor, delegate, and empower growth.

8. Adaptability

Essence:

Adjusting quickly to change and uncertainty.

Impact:

Adaptable leaders remain effective in shifting environments.

Expression:

They embrace change as opportunity, not threat.

9. Integrity in Action

Essence:

Leading ethically, honestly, and consistently.

Impact:

Integrity sustains credibility and trust.

Expression:

Leaders model what they expect.

10. Time and Priority Management

Essence:

Focusing energy on what matters most.

Impact:

Time mastery increases productivity and reduces burnout.

Expression:
Leaders prioritize purpose over pressure.

DEVELOPING LEADERSHIP SKILLS

Effective leaders are not born — they are built.

Growth Pathways:

- Commit to continuous learning
- Seek honest feedback
- Practice leadership in real environments
- Reflect on successes and failures
- Learn from mentors and coaches

Leadership ability expands through intentional practice.

THE LION METAPHOR — LEADERSHIP IN NATURE

The lion is called king of the jungle not because it is the biggest, fastest, or smartest — but because of how it leads.

Lion Leadership Lessons:

- **Courage** — faces challenges boldly
- **Confidence** — commands respect naturally
- **Strategic Vision** — plans before acting
- **Decisiveness** — acts with precision
- **Teamwork** — leads the pride effectively

- **Resilience** — rises after setbacks

Lesson:

Leadership is not about superiority — it is about mastery of presence, strategy, and influence.

CONCLUSION

Leadership skills turn character into competence. Vision without skill remains imagination. Skill without character becomes manipulation. True leadership unites both.

When leaders develop communication, emotional intelligence, decision-making, adaptability, and strategic thinking, they unlock extraordinary capacity in themselves and in others.

Leadership is not what you know.

It is what you can consistently do. With these skills established, we now explore the different leadership styles and how they are applied.

KEY TAKEAWAYS

- Leadership requires developed abilities
- Communication creates alignment
- Emotional intelligence builds trust
- Strategic thinking sustains direction
- Problem-solving overcomes obstacles
- Adaptability ensures relevance
- Skillful leaders multiply impact

REFLECTION QUESTIONS

1. Which leadership skill is your greatest strength?

2. Which skill needs focus improvement?

3. How well do you listen before speaking?

4. Are your decisions timely or delayed?

5. How do you handle conflict?

6. Are you leading strategically or reactively?

7. What leadership skills will define your next growth season?

Write your reflections. Awareness unlocks advancement.

ACTION STEPS

1. Identify one leadership skill to strengthen this month.

2. Ask your team for honest feedback.

3. Practice active listening daily.

4. Make one strategic decision this week.

5. Read one book on leadership competence.

6. Mentor someone to reinforce your skill.

7. Reflect weekly on your leadership execution.

Skill grows by repetition.

CLOSING THOUGHT

Vision shows the destination.

Character sets the foundation.

Skill builds the bridge.

Cross wisely.

Champion Remain.

CHAPTER 23 — Leadership Styles

"The best leaders do not use one style — they use the right style at the right time." — **John C. Maxwell**

Introduction

Leadership is not one-size-fits-all. Different people, situations, cultures, and challenges require different approaches. A wise leader understands that effectiveness is not found in clinging to one leadership style but in mastering multiple styles and applying them appropriately.

Leadership maturity is revealed not in knowing styles — but in knowing **when** to use them.

This chapter explores the major leadership styles, their strengths, their limitations, and the environments where they function best — equipping you to lead with flexibility and wisdom.

THE MAJOR LEADERSHIP STYLES

1. Autocratic Leadership

Essence:

The leader makes decisions independently and gives direct instructions.

Strength:

Fast, clear, decisive control — essential in emergencies.

Limitation:

Can suppress creativity and lower morale if overused.

Best Used When:

- Crisis situations

- Military operations

- High-risk or safety-critical environments

Example:

Winston Churchill's decisive wartime leadership kept Britain unified during World War II.

Lesson:

Autocratic leadership saves time — but must be balanced with wisdom.

2. Democratic Leadership

Essence:

The leader involves team members in decision-making.

Strength:

Builds engagement, creativity, and ownership.

Limitation:

Decision-making may be slow when urgency is required.

Best Used When:

- Innovative environments

- Educational institutions

- Collaborative corporate cultures

Example:

Google's participative culture has produced world-changing innovations.

Lesson:

Inclusion strengthens commitment.

3. Transformational Leadership

Essence:

The leader inspires people toward a shared vision.

Strength:

Creates passion, unity, and extraordinary performance.

Limitation:

Requires emotional stamina and strong communication ability.

Best Used When:

- Startups

- Change-driven organizations

- Visionary movements

Example:

Steve Jobs transformed Apple by inspiring bold imagination.

Lesson:

Vision ignites transformation.

4. Transactional Leadership

Essence:

Leadership through structured rewards and accountability.

Strength:

Produces consistent performance and measurable results.

Limitation:

Does not inspire long-term passion or innovation.

Best Used When:

- Sales organizations

- Performance-based environments

- Operational Systems

Example:

Retail and service industries commonly use transactional motivation models.

Lesson:

Rewards drive output — but vision drives purpose.

5. Laissez-Faire Leadership

Essence:

The leader grants high autonomy to skilled teams.

Strength:

Encourages creativity and independence.

Limitation:

Fails when teams lack discipline or direction.

Best Used When:

Research teams

Creative industries

Expert-driven organizations

Example:

Warren Buffett allows managers, full operational autonomy at Berkshire Hathaway.

Lesson:

Freedom works best with maturity.

6. Servant Leadership

Essence:

The leader serves the team first.

Strength:

Builds loyalty, trust, and people-centered culture.

Limitation:

Can be misinterpreted as weak if balance is lost.

Best Used When:

- Faith-based organizations

- Healthcare

- Non-profit institutions

Example:

Howard Schultz built Starbucks through employee-first leadership.

Lesson:

Serving others multiply influence.

THE ADAPTIVE LEADER'S SECRET

Great leaders do not ask: "What is my style-"

They ask: "What does this moment require-"

Leadership excellence lies in **style agility**.

CONCLUSION

Leadership styles are tools — not identities. An effective leader masters' multiple styles and applies them wisely.

Rigid leadership breaks under pressure. Adaptive leadership thrives in complexity.

The leader who grows in flexibility grows in influence. Understanding leadership styles now prepares us to explore the challenges leaders face and how they overcome them.

KEY TAKEAWAYS

- No single leadership style fits all situations
- Autocratic leadership provides decisive control
- Democratic leadership builds engagement
- Transformational leadership inspires greatness
- Transactional leadership ensures consistency
- Laissez-faire leadership empowers experts
- Servant leadership builds loyalty
- Adaptive leaders master all styles

REFLECTION QUESTIONS

1. What leadership style do you use most naturally?

2. Which style challenges you the most?

3. When was a different style needed but not applied?

4. Does your team need more direction or more autonomy?

5. How flexible is your leadership approach?

6. Which leadership style will you practice this month?

7. What environment are you called to lead in now?

Reflection reveals readiness.

ACTION STEPS

1. Identify your dominant leadership style.

2. Ask your team how they experience your leadership.

3. Practice a new style in one meeting this week.

4. Observe leaders who use styles different from yours.

5. Study situational leadership principles.

6. Journal weekly about leadership adjustments.

7. Lead with awareness, not habit.

Flexibility is leadership maturity.

CLOSING THOUGHT

The strength of a leader is not in one style, but in the wisdom to choose the right style at the right time. **Champion Remain.**

PART IV — LEADERSHIP CHALLENGES & SOLUTIONS

A leader stands firm under pressure.

CHAPTER 24 — The Downfall of Leaders: Why Great Leaders Fall or Fail

"Pride goeth before destruction, and a haughty spirit before a fall."

— Proverbs 16:18

Introduction

Leadership is a high calling — and a high-risk assignment. The higher a leader rises, the farther they can fall.

History, Scripture, and modern society all testify to one truth: **No leader is immune to failure.**

Understanding why leaders fall is not meant to instill fear — but to cultivate wisdom, humility, and vigilance.

Those who learn from the fall of others do not have to repeat the same mistakes.

THE REALITY OF LEADERSHIP FAILURE

Many leaders believe failure happens to others — until it happens to them.

From politics to business, from ministry to sports, high-profile downfalls remind us that success does not equal immunity.

Giftedness may open doors. Character keeps them open.

LESSONS FROM PUBLIC DOWNFALLS

History is filled with gifted leaders who fell because their private life contradicted their public image.

- Political leaders destroyed by scandal
- Business leaders ruined by greed
- Ministers exposed by moral compromise
- Celebrities undone by unchecked appetite

Their stories reveal a sobering truth:

Talent can take you to the top — but only character keeps you there.

PERSONAL FAILURES — LESSONS LEARNED

Every seasoned leader eventually discovers:
Some of the greatest leadership lessons come from personal missteps.

Common leadership mistakes include:

- Ignoring early warning signs
- Overextending into too many projects
- Failing to set boundaries
- Neglecting important details
- Avoiding difficult decisions
- Trying to please everyone
- Rushing major decisions
- Poor record keeping

- Delayed action

- Weak communication

Each mistake is small in the beginning — but left unchecked, small cracks become structural collapse.

CONSEQUENCES OF LEADERSHIP FAILURE

Leadership failure rarely affects only the leader.

It often produces:

- Financial loss

- Broken relationships

- Emotional stress

- Public embarrassment

- Loss of confidence

- Lost opportunities

- Family strain

- Starting over from scratch

The cost of failure is always higher than the cost of discipline.

WARNING SIGNS OF A LEADER IN DANGER

1. **Distraction** — Losing focus on core mission

2. **Poor Communication** — Vision becomes unclear

3. **Lack of Boldness** — Fear replaces courage

4. **Ethical Compromise** — Small moral shortcuts

5. **Poor Self-Management** — Neglect of rest and renewal

6. **Loss of Passion** — Vision no longer burns

A leader who ignores warning signs eventually faces consequences.

THE THREE ROOT CAUSES OF LEADERSHIP FAILURE

Scripture identifies three timeless traps:

1. **Pride** — "I am above accountability."

2. **Lust** — Uncontrolled appetite for sex, power, or pleasure.

3. **Greed** — Love of money and status.

These three forces have toppled kings, presidents, CEOs, and pastors alike.

Unchecked desire always leads to collapse.

ESTABLISHING BOUNDARIES TO PREVENT FAILURE

Wise leaders build protective systems before temptation appears.

1. Honest Advisors

Surround yourself with people who can challenge you, not flatter you.

2. Spiritual Grounding

Remain connected to God through prayer, Scripture, and humility.

3. Servant's Heart

Remember: leadership is stewardship, not ownership.

4. Personal Discipline

Guard time, energy, integrity, and reputation.

Boundaries are not limitations — they are leadership insurance.

CONCLUSION

Leadership failure is not sudden. It is the final chapter of many ignored warnings.

But leaders who remain teachable, humble, accountable, and spiritually grounded can rise, lead, and finish well.

The goal is not simply to succeed — but to **finish strong with integrity intact**. Understanding why leaders fail now leads us to explore whether leadership is innate or developed.

KEY TAKEAWAYS

- No leader is immune to failure
- Character sustains success

- Small compromises lead to major collapse

- Pride, lust, and greed remain timeless dangers

- Warning signs must not be ignored

- Boundaries protect destiny

- Accountability preserves leadership longevity

REFLECTION QUESTIONS

1. What warning signs do I recognize in myself?

2. Where am I most vulnerable — pride, desire, or greed?

3. Who has permission to correct me?

4. Have I built enough personal boundaries?

5. How do I manage rest, stress, and renewal?

6. What discipline must I strengthen this season?

7. What legacy do I want to protect?

Reflection prevents destruction.

ACTION STEPS

1. Identify one vulnerability area this week.

2. Establish one new accountability relationship.

3. Create personal leadership boundaries.

4. Schedule weekly self-examination time.

5. Review vision and motivation monthly.

6. Practice saying "no" when necessary.

7. Pray daily for humility and wisdom.

Small disciplines preserve great destinies.

Closing Thought

Great leaders are not those who never fall — but those who walk humbly enough to never fall beyond recovery. Finish well.
Guard your calling.

Champion Remain.

CHAPTER 25 — Are Leaders Born or Made?

"You don't have to be great to start, but you have to start to be great." — Zig Ziglar

Introduction

Few questions in leadership spark more debate than this: **Are leaders born, or are leaders made-**

Some seem to emerge naturally — confident, charismatic, and influential from an early age. Others grow into leadership through learning, hardship, mentorship, and persistence.

The truth is not found in extremes. Leadership is neither purely inherited nor purely constructed. It is **potentially refined through process**.

THE CASE FOR BORN LEADERS

Some individuals possess natural tendencies that make leadership come more easily.

Common inborn leadership traits include:

- **Charisma** — Natural ability to attract and influence others

- **Confidence** — Inner assurance that inspires trust

- **Decisiveness** — Quick, instinctive judgment

- **Empathy** — Natural sensitivity to people

- **Visionary Thinking** — Ability to see possibilities beyond the present

These traits provide an early advantage. But raw talent
without discipline never produces lasting leadership.

Giftedness opens doors. Development determines how long
you stay inside.

THE CASE FOR MADE LEADERS

Leadership can absolutely be learned. Many of history's
greatest leaders were not natural-born influencers — they
became leaders through:

- Training

- Experience

- Mentorship

- Failure

- Self-reflection

- Deliberate practice

Skills that can be developed include:

- Communication

- Emotional intelligence

- Strategic thinking

- Conflict management

- Decision-making

- Adaptability

Leadership is a muscle — unused, it weakens; trained, it
strengthens.

THE REALITY: LEADERS ARE BOTH BORN AND MADE

Most leadership experts now agree:

Leaders are born with potential — but made through process.

- Natural traits give early advantage
- Learned skills refine effectiveness
- Experience builds wisdom
- Feedback sharpens character
- Self-discipline sustains growth

Even the most naturally gifted leader must learn. Even the least confident beginner can grow.

Leadership is not a destination. It is a lifelong construction project.

LEADERSHIP AS A PROCESS

Effective leadership unfolds through:

1. Learning by Doing

Leadership is perfected in practice, not theory.

2. Mentorship and Modeling

Great leaders are shaped by greater leaders.

3. Feedback and Reflection

Self-awareness accelerates growth.

4. Training and Education

Knowledge strengthens capacity.

5. Personal Initiative

No one develops a leader who refuses to grow.

CONCLUSION

The question is not whether leaders are born or made.

The real question is:

Will you develop leadership potential within you-

Natural talent without growth remains dormant. Learned skill without character collapses.

But when potential meets discipline — great leadership emerges.

Leadership is not reserved for a chosen few. It is available to all who commit to growth. This understanding now prepares us to examine the attitudes that shape effective leadership.

KEY TAKEAWAYS

- Some leadership traits are natural
- Leadership skills can be learned
- Potential must be developed
- Experience shapes effectiveness
- Growth requires intentional effort
- Leadership is a lifelong journey

REFLECTION QUESTIONS

1. What natural leadership traits do I possess?

2. Which leadership skills must I develop further?

3. Who has shaped my leadership journey?

4. What experiences have taught me the most?

5. Am I actively investing in my growth?

6. What leadership skills will I develop this season?

7. What kind of leader am I becoming?

ACTION STEPS

1. Identify one leadership strength to maximize.

2. Identify one leadership weakness to develop.

3. Seek a mentor or leadership role model.

4. Schedule weekly leadership learning time.

5. Request feedback from trusted peers.

6. Practice leadership in small opportunities.

7. Commit to continuous improvement.

CLOSING THOUGHT

You may be born with potential. But you become a leader by choice.

Leadership is not inherited — it is built.

CHAPTER 26 — The Attitude of Leadership

"Attitude is a little thing that makes a big difference." — Winston Churchill

Introduction

Leadership is not sustained by knowledge alone. It is not defined by skills alone. It is powered by **attitude**.

A leader's attitude determines the emotional climate of the organization, the morale of the team, and the endurance of the vision. Skills may open doors. Knowledge may provide tools. But attitude determines how those tools are used.

The most influential leaders in history were not always the most gifted, but they consistently carried the **right mindset, emotional posture, and spirit**.

WHAT IS LEADERSHIP ATTITUDE-

Leadership attitude is the mental and emotional approach a leader adopts toward people, responsibilities, challenges, and opportunities. It shapes how leaders interpret situations, respond under pressure, and influence others.

A positive leadership attitude produces confidence, creativity, and commitment.
A negative attitude breeds fear, disengagement, and stagnation.

Attitude is the inner climate that creates the outer culture.

THE IMPORTANCE OF LEADERSHIP ATTITUDE

1. Influence on Team Morale

Teams mirror their leaders. Encouraging leaders produce motivated teams. Discouraged leaders create discouraged environments.

2. Shaping Organizational Culture

Culture is leadership attitude repeated daily.

3. Resilience in the Face of Challenges

Attitude determines whether obstacles become barriers or breakthroughs.

4. Enhancing Leadership Effectiveness

People follow leaders whose presence lifts them rather than drains them.

KEY ATTITUDES OF SUCCESSFUL LEADERS

Positivity

Seeing possibilities instead of limitations.

Resilience

Bouncing forward after setbacks.

Empathy

Understanding hearts, not just tasks.

Adaptability

Flexibility in changing environments.

Humility

Serving rather than seeking status.

Optimism

Expecting progress even in difficulty.

Integrity

Doing right even when unseen.

These attitudes form the **inner character of enduring leadership**.

THE POWER OF THE RIGHT ATTITUDE

"Nothing can stop the person with the right mental attitude from achieving their goal." — Thomas Jefferson

"People may hear your words, but they feel your attitude." — John C. Maxwell

Attitude speaks louder than instruction.

DEVELOPING A GREAT ATTITUDE

A great attitude is a crucial success factor — equating to **100% leadership effectiveness**. This truth can be illustrated through a simple perspective:

$$H+A+R+D+W+O+R+K = 98\%$$
$$K+N+O+W+L+E+D+G+E = 96\%$$
$$L+O+V+E = 54\%$$
$$L+U+C+K = 47\%$$
$$A+T+T+I+T+U+D+E = 100\%$$

This formula demonstrates that while hard work, knowledge, and luck are important, **the right attitude is what ultimately leads to total success**.

DEVELOPING THE RIGHT ATTITUDES FOR LEADERSHIP

Effective leadership requires attitudes that earn respect and inspire others to follow.

Genuine Interest in People

Great leaders genuinely care about people. They remember names.
They ask about personal and professional growth. They offer support when needed.

People do not follow leaders who use them — they follow leaders who value them.

Fairness

Fair leaders treat everyone with respect and impartiality.
They offer equal opportunity for recognition and growth.
They build environments where every team member feels valued.

Fairness builds trust. Trust builds loyalty.

CULTIVATING A POWERFUL LEADERSHIP ATTITUDE

1. Self-Awareness

Monitor your inner dialogue — it becomes your leadership tone.

2. Continuous Learning

A growth mindset sustains a healthy attitude.

3. Positive Associations

Surround yourself with voices that stretch you forward.

4. Gratitude Practice

Gratitude fuels optimism and emotional stability.

5. Leading by Example

Attitudes taught are forgotten. Attitudes modeled are
multiplied.

ATTITUDE AS A DAILY CHOICE

Leadership attitude is not inherited — it is chosen daily.

You cannot control events. You can always control your
response.

That response becomes your leadership identity.

BIBLICAL FOUNDATION

"Fixing our eyes on Jesus… For the joy set before Him, He
endured the cross." — Hebrews 12:2

Purpose-driven attitude sustains endurance.

CONCLUSION

Skills can be learned. Knowledge can be acquired.
But **attitude must be chosen**. A leader with average skill
and great attitude will outperform a leader with great skill
and poor attitude.

Attitude is the invisible force that unlocks leadership destiny.
With the right attitude in place, we now explore the
challenges leaders face in real-world situations.

KEY TAKEAWAYS

- Attitude shapes leadership climate

- Teams reflect leader's mindset

- Culture flows from repeated attitude

- Resilience is attitude under pressure

- Right attitude multiplies influence

- Attitude is a daily decision

REFLECTION QUESTIONS

1. What attitude do I project daily?

2. How do people feel after interacting with me?

3. How do I respond under pressure?

4. What attitude must I change today?

5. Who models the attitude I desire?

ACTION STEPS

1. Choose your attitude each morning.

2. Replace complaints with gratitude.

3. Speak hope into difficult situations.

4. Encourage someone daily.

5. Reflect nightly on attitude moments.

Closing Thought

Leadership begins in the heart. Attitude reveals the heart. And the heart shapes the legacy.

Choose your attitude — and you choose your future.

CHAPTER 27 — The Challenges of Leadership

"Leaders don't wait. They shape their own frontiers. The bigger the challenge, the greater the opportunity."

Introduction

Leadership is rewarding — but never easy.

Every leader who rises to significance encounters resistance, pressure, uncertainty, criticism, and complexity. Challenges are not signs of failure; they are **proof that leadership is in motion**.

As Jim Loehr observed:

"The ability to summon positive emotions during periods of intense stress lies at the heart of effective leadership."

Great leaders are not those who avoid challenges. They are those who **transform challenges into platforms for growth, wisdom, and influence**.

UNDERSTANDING LEADERSHIP CHALLENGES

A leadership challenge is any obstacle, pressure, or complexity that tests a leader's judgment, resilience, emotional intelligence, and character. Challenges arise from:

- People
- Systems
- Change
- Uncertainty

- Personal limitations

- External forces

Mastering leadership means mastering the navigation of these challenges.

TWENTY MAJOR CHALLENGES OF LEADERSHIP AND STRATEGIES TO OVERCOME THEM

1. Managing Change

Change is inevitable — resistance is predictable.

Strategies:

- Communicate vision clearly

- Show empathy to concerns

- Plan transitions strategically

2. Building and Motivating Teams

Diverse personalities and expectations require intentional unity.

Strategies:

- Build trust

- Foster collaboration

- Provide clear direction

3. Decision-Making Under Uncertainty

Leaders often decide without complete information.

Strategies:

- Use decision frameworks

- Seek counsel

- Act with courage

4. Managing Conflict

Conflict can destroy or develop — depending on leadership.

Strategies:

- Practice active listening

- Mediate fairly

- Maintain dignity in dialogue

5. Strategic Planning and Execution

Vision without execution is hallucination.

Strategies:

- Align short-term action with long-term vision

- Prioritize effectively

- Stay adaptable

6. Crisis Management

Pressure reveals leadership maturity.

Strategies:

- Prepare crisis plans

- Communicate transparently

- Act decisively

7. Embracing Diversity and Inclusion

Diversity fuels innovation — exclusion kills it.

Strategies:

- Promote equity

- Create inclusive environments

- Address bias intentionally

8. Self-Leadership and Personal Development

You cannot lead others beyond where you lead yourself.

Strategies:

- Practice self-awareness

- Commit to lifelong learning

- Maintain work-life balance

9. Inspiring and Sustaining Motivation

Motivation leaks — leaders must refill it.

Strategies:

- Recognize effort

- Connect work to purpose

- Empower ownership

10. Navigating Organizational Politics

Politics unmanaged becomes poison.

Strategies:

- Build alliances

- Stay neutral

- Operate transparently

11. Succession Planning

True leaders build replacements, not dependence.

Strategies:

- Mentor emerging leaders

- Identify talent early

- Create transition plans

12. Maintaining Innovation

Comfort kills creativity.

Strategies:

- Encourage experimentation

- Reward ideas

- Promote learning culture

13. Cultural Integration

Unified vision must honor diverse identity.

Strategies:

- Promote cultural awareness

- Establish shared values

- Practice inclusive leadership

14. Managing Remote Teams

Distance demands trust.

Strategies:

- Communicate consistently

- Use collaboration tools

- Set clear expectations

15. Sustaining Employee Engagement

Engagement is emotional, not mechanical.

Strategies:

- Offer development paths

- Recognize contributions

- Support well-being

16. Balancing Autonomy and Control

Micromanagement kills momentum. Neglect kills alignment.

Strategies:

- Set clear guidelines

- Delegate wisely

- Maintain feedback loops

17. Managing Organizational Growth

Growth without structure breeds chaos.

Strategies:

- Build scalable systems

- Recruit strategically

- Preserve core culture

18. Ensuring Financial Stability

Vision must rest on financial discipline.

Strategies:

- Practice financial planning

- Control costs

- Diversify revenue

19. Handling Public and Media Scrutiny

Reputation is leadership currency.

Strategies:

- Communicate proactively
- Manage crises professionally
- Lead ethically always

20. Fostering a Learning Organization

Organizations grow only as fast as their learning.

Strategies:

- Invest in training

- Encourage knowledge sharing

- Develop leaders at every level

THE 18 PERSONAL LEADERSHIP CHALLENGES

1. The Proactive Challenge
2. The Influence Challenge
3. The Reality Challenge
4. The Vision Challenge
5. The Strategy Challenge
6. The Wisdom Challenge
7. The Insight Challenge
8. The Confidence Challenge
9. The Internal Compass Challenge
10. The Growth Challenge
11. The Vertigo Challenge
12. The Delegation Challenge
13. The Transition Challenge

14. The Loneliness Challenge

15. The Personality Challenge

16. The Blind Spot Challenge

17. The Complexity Challenge

18. The Work-Life Balance Challenge

These challenges shape maturity, depth, and endurance in leadership.

CONCLUSION

Leadership challenges are unavoidable. Leadership failure is optional.

As John R. Miller wisely said:

"If you call your troubles experiences and remember that every experience develops some latent force within you, you will grow vigorous and happy, however adverse your circumstances may seem."

Challenges are leadership classrooms. Graduates become legacy leaders. Understanding these challenges now leads us to examine the leadership process in action. Understanding these challenges now leads us to examine the leadership process in action.

KEY TAKEAWAYS

- Challenges confirm leadership growth

- Resistance reveals readiness

- Crisis exposes character

- Change demands courage

- People require emotional intelligence

- Strategy demands adaptability

- Self-leadership precedes people leadership

REFLECTION QUESTIONS

1. Which leadership challenge do I face most often?

2. How do I currently respond under pressure?

3. Which challenge can become my next growth breakthrough?

4. Who mentors me through leadership difficulty?

5. What challenge is preparing me for my next level?

ACTION STEPS

1. Identify your top three leadership challenges.

2. Write one strategy for overcoming each.

3. Seek counsel from an experienced leader.

4. Commit to continuous personal development.

5. View every challenge as leadership training.

CLOSING THOUGHT

Leadership is not proven by comfort. Leadership is revealed by challenge.

Embrace the challenge — and you embrace your destiny as a legacy leader.

CHAPTER 28 — The Leadership Process

"Leadership is not a position. Leadership is a process."

Introduction

Leadership is not merely a trait, a talent, or a title.
It is a **living, moving, evolving process**.

Every effective leader continuously guides, influences, motivates, evaluates, adjusts, and grows. Leadership is never static — it is dynamic, relational, and developmental.

The leadership process is how vision becomes action, how intention becomes impact, and how people become aligned toward purpose.

This chapter explores the **core stages of the leadership process**, the **development journey of a leader**, and the **role followers play** in achieving shared success.

THE LEADERSHIP PROCESS DEFINED

The leadership process is the systematic cycle through which a leader:

- Understands reality

- Defines direction

- Communicates vision

- Makes decisions

- Mobilizes action

- Monitors progress

- Adapts continuously

This process repeats continually. Great leaders do not complete the process — they **live** it.

THE SEVEN CORE STAGES OF THE LEADERSHIP PROCESS

1. Understanding the Situation

Leadership begins with awareness.

Effective leaders assess:

- Internal conditions

- External environments

- Team strengths and weaknesses

- Opportunities and threats

Clarity precedes direction.

2. Setting Vision and Goals

Vision gives meaning. Goals give measurement.

Leaders:

- Define compelling vision

- Align it with mission and values

- Establish SMART goals

- Connect individual roles to collective purpose

Vision attracts commitment.

3. Communication and Influence

Vision unspoken remains imagination.

Leaders must:

- Communicate clearly
- Listen actively
- Inspire belief
- Build trust
- Create ownership

Influence multiplies effort.

4. Decision-Making

Leaders turn uncertainty into direction.

Effective decision-making requires:

- Gathering information
- Evaluating alternatives
- Considering consequences
- Acting decisively
- Remaining flexible

Delay is also a decision.

5. Implementation and Action

Plans without execution produce frustration.

Leaders:

- Assign responsibility
- Provide resources
- Remove obstacles

- Monitor momentum

- Encourage accountability

Execution validates leadership.

6. Monitoring and Feedback

What gets measured improves.

Leaders:

- Track progress

- Provide feedback

- Reinforce success

- Correct deviation

- Celebrate milestones

Feedback fuels alignment.

7. Adaptation and Continuous Improvement

Leadership remains effective only through adaptation.

Leaders:

- Learn from experience

- Adjust strategy

- Embrace change

- Foster innovation

- Grow continuously

Adaptability sustains relevance.

THE LEADERSHIP DEVELOPMENT PROCESS

Leadership is not achieved — it is developed.

As John C. Maxwell teaches:

"Leadership develops daily, not in a day."

THE FIVE STAGES OF LEADERSHIP GROWTH

Stage 1 — Unaware

"I don't know what I don't know."

Stage 2 — Discovery

"I know I need to learn leadership."

Stage 3 — Awareness

"I know what I must develop."

Stage 4 — Application

"I grow, and it shows."

Stage 5 — mastery

"I lead naturally through practiced wisdom."

Progression requires intentional growth.

DAILY COMMITMENT TO LEADERSHIP GROWTH

Great leaders' practice:

- Reading daily
- Reflecting regularly
- Seeking mentorship
- Applying lessons
- Serving consistently

The process matters more than the event.

THE ROLE OF FOLLOWERS IN THE

- Provide feedback
- Offer ideas
- Strengthen execution
- Share ownership
- Multiply results

LEADERSHIP PROCESS

Leadership is relational, not positional.

Followers:

Empowered followers create sustainable leadership.

CHALLENGES WITHIN THE LEADERSHIP PROCESS

Leaders encounter:

- Resistance
- Resource constraints
- Uncertainty
- Competing priorities
- Human complexity

Process discipline transforms challenge into progress.

CONCLUSION

Leadership is a continuous cycle:

Understand → Vision → Communicate → Decide → Act → Monitor → Adapt.

Those who master the process master leadership.

Leadership is not what you do once, it is what you practice consistently. With a clear understanding of the process, we now explore common myths that distort leadership.

KEY TAKEAWAYS

- Leadership is a continuous process
- Awareness precedes action
- Vision directs movement
- Communication creates alignment
- Execution validates leadership
- Feedback sustains improvement
- Adaptability ensures longevity

REFLECTION QUESTIONS

1. Which stage of the leadership process do I excel in most?

2. Where do I need the greatest improvement?

3. How clearly do I communicate vision?

4. Do I execute as strongly as I plan?

5. How open am I to feedback and adaptation?

ACTION STEPS

1. Evaluate your current leadership process.

2. Strengthen your weakest stage.

3. Create a personal daily growth plan.

4. Seek feedback from your team.

5. Practice continuous improvement intentionally.

CLOSING THOUGHT

Leadership is not an event. It is a practiced process.

Master the process — and you will multiply your influence.

CHAPTER 29 — Leadership Myths

"The greatest obstacle to leadership growth is not lack of knowledge — it is believing what is not true."

Introduction

Leadership has been studied for centuries. Yet despite the abundance of research, teaching, and experience, many **false beliefs** about leadership still persist.

These leadership myths create unrealistic expectations, discourage emerging leaders, and distort what effective leadership truly requires.

This chapter exposes the most common leadership myths, replaces them with truth, and equips leaders to walk in **clarity, confidence, and authenticity**.

MYTH 1 — LEADERS ARE BORN, NOT MADE

Myth: Only a few are born leaders.

Truth: Leadership is developed, not inherited.

While some may possess natural traits, effective leadership is built through:

- Learning
- Practice
- Experience
- Personal growth

As Warren Bennis said:

"Leaders are made rather than born."

Leadership potential exists in everyone willing to grow.

MYTH 2 — LEADERSHIP REQUIRES CHARISMA

Myth: Only charismatic personalities can lead.

Truth: Character outweighs charisma.

Many powerful leaders:

- Are quiet
- Are thoughtful
- Lead through integrity
- Influence through trust

Charisma may attract attention — but character sustains influence.

MYTH 3 — THE PERSON WITH THE TITLE IS THE LEADER

Myth: Position equals leadership.

Truth: Influence defines leadership.

Leadership happens at:

- Every level
- Every team
- Every organization

A title may give authority — but influence earns followership.

MYTH 4 — LEADERSHIP IS ABOUT CONTROL AND POWER

Myth: Leaders control people.

Truth: Leaders empower people.

True leadership:

- Serves

- Develops

- Guides

- Releases potential

Control limits growth. Empowerment multiplies strength.

MYTH 5 — GOOD LEADERS NEVER SHOW VULNERABILITY

Myth: Leaders must appear invincible.

Truth: Authenticity builds trust.

Great leaders:

- Admit mistakes

- Show empathy

- Remain human

- Create psychological safety

Vulnerability is not weakness — it is credibility.

MYTH 6 — LEADERSHIP IS THE SAME IN EVERY SITUATION

Myth: One style fits all.

Truth: Leadership is situational.

Effective leaders:

- Read context

- Adapt approach

- Adjust style

- Respond wisely

Flexibility distinguishes mature leadership.

MYTH 7 — LEADERSHIP IS ALL ABOUT RESULTS

Myth: Only outcomes matter.

Truth: Methods matter as much as results.

Sustainable leadership balances:

- Performance
- Ethics
- People
- Purpose

Results without integrity create collapse.

MYTH 8 — LEADERSHIP CANNOT BE LEARNED

Myth: You either have it or you don't.

Truth: Leadership is teachable.

Leadership grows through:

- Training
- Mentorship
- Reflection
- Practice

Anyone willing to grow can lead effectively.

MYTH 9 — GOOD LEADERS HAVE MORE EDUCATION

Myth: Degrees create leaders.

Truth: Wisdom and experience create leaders.

Education informs leadership — but emotional intelligence, experience, and integrity define it.

Some of history's greatest leaders had little formal education — yet enormous influence.

CONCLUSION

Leadership myths distort reality. Truth liberates potential.

Leadership is not:

- Title
- Charisma
- Control
- Perfection
- Inherited talent

Leadership is:

- Influence
- Growth
- Service
- Adaptability
- Character

When leaders reject myths, they lead freely and authentically. Dispelling these myths now prepares us to clearly distinguish between a boss and a true leader.

KEY TAKEAWAYS

- Leadership is developed, not inherited

- Influence matters more than position

- Character outweighs charisma

- Vulnerability builds trust

- Leadership adapts to situations

- Ethics matter as much as results

- Anyone willing to grow can lead

REFLECTION QUESTIONS

1. Which leadership myth have I believed in the past?

2. How has that belief limited my leadership growth?

3. Where can I shift from control to empowerment?

4. Do I lead from title or influence?

5. How can I lead more authentically this season?

ACTION STEPS

1. Identify one leadership myth to permanently reject.

2. Replace it with a leadership truth.

3. Practice influences without relying on position.

4. Show authentic vulnerability with your team.

5. Commit to continuous leadership learning.

CLOSING THOUGHT

Leadership is not what myths say it is. Leadership is who you become through growth, service, and influence.

Reject the myths. Embrace the process. Build your legacy.

CHAPTER 30 — Boss vs. Leader

"A boss creates compliance. A leader creates commitment."

Introduction

In the workplace, the words *boss* and *leader* are often used interchangeably. Yet they represent two entirely different approaches to guiding people.

A boss manages through authority. A leader mobilizes through influence.

Understanding this distinction is crucial for anyone who desires to build motivated teams, healthy organizational cultures, and sustainable success.

This chapter explores the differences between a boss and a leader, the cultural impact of each, and the practical steps required to transition from being a boss to becoming a true leader.

Defining Boss vs. Leader

Boss: A boss holds a position of authority and directs people primarily through control, rules, and compliance. The relationship is often transactional — "do this because I said so."

Leader: A leader inspires, influences, and empowers people toward a shared vision. The relationship is relational — "let's accomplish this together."

A boss drives performance. A leader develops people.

KEY DIFFERENCES BETWEEN A BOSS AND A LEADER

1. Authority vs. Influence

Boss: Uses positional power to command.

Leader: Uses earned influence to inspire.

Authority demands obedience. Influence invites commitment.

2. Commands vs. Inspires

Boss: Gives orders.

Leader: Communicates vision.

A boss says,"*Do this.*" A leader says *"Here's why these matters."*

3. Controls vs. Empowers

Boss: Micromanages to maintain control.

Leader: Delegates to develop capacity.

Control limits growth. Empowerment multiplies potential.

4. Blames vs. Takes Responsibility

Boss: Looks for who is at fault.

Leader: Looks for how to improve.

Blame creates fear. Ownership creates trust.

5. Criticizes vs. Encourages

Boss: Highlights failure.

Leader: Cultivates progress.

Criticism drains morale. Encouragement fuels excellence.

6. Short-Term Focus vs. Long-Term Vision

Boss: Focuses on immediate results.

Leader: Builds sustainable success.

A boss meets deadlines. A leader builds destiny.

7. Enforces Rules vs. Builds Culture

Boss: Enforces compliance.

Leader: Shapes values.

Rules maintain order. Culture drives excellence.

8. Demands Respect vs. Earns Respect

Boss: Requires respect by title.

Leader: Receives respect by character.

Fear obeys. Respect follows.

THE CULTURAL IMPACT

Boss-Led Culture

- Fear-based compliance
- Low morale
- Minimal innovation
- High turnover
- Short-term productivity only

Leader-Led Culture

- Trust-based engagement
- High motivation
- Innovation and creativity
- Strong loyalty
- Long-term sustainability

The difference between the two determines whether an organization merely survives — or truly thrives.

TRANSITIONING FROM BOSS TO LEADER

Becoming a leader is a decision, not a promotion.

1. Develop Self-Awareness

- Reflect honestly on your leadership style
- Invite feedback
- Identify control tendencies

2. Build Relationships

- Know your people personally
- Be approachable
- Create trust

3. Shift from Control to Empowerment

- Delegate authority
- Trust competence
- Support autonomy

4. Communicate Vision

- Paint the bigger picture
- Connect daily tasks to purpose

5. Practice Emotional Intelligence

- Listen actively
- Show empathy
- Respond wisely

6. Encourage Growth

- Provide learning opportunities

- Recognize progress

- Celebrate achievements

7. **Lead by Example**

- Model integrity

- Demonstrate accountability

- Serve alongside your team

QUOTES ON BOSS VS. LEADER

"A boss fixes blame. A leader fixes breakdown." — Russell H. Ewing

"A boss says 'Go. ' A leader says, 'Let's go. '" — E. M. Kelly

"The best bosses aren't bosses — they are leaders." — Charles Erwin Wilson

CONCLUSION

A boss may achieve compliance. A leader achieves commitment.

A boss controls people. A leader grows people.

A boss demands results. A leader builds legacy.

Every boss can become a leader — not by changing position, but by changing approach. With this distinction in mind, we now move into advanced leadership insights that deepen understanding and effectiveness.

KEY TAKEAWAYS

- Authority commands; influence inspires

- Control limits; empowerment multiplies

- Blame weakens; responsibility strengthens

- Rules manage; culture transforms

- Titles give power; character gives leadership

REFLECTION QUESTIONS

1. In which situations do I act more like a boss than a leader?

2. How do my team members experience my leadership?

3. Where can I shift from control to empowerment this week?

4. What behavior must I change to earn deeper respect?

5. What kind of culture am I creating?

ACTION STEPS

1. Ask one team member for honest feedback.

2. Delegate one responsibility you normally control.

3. Share your vision more clearly this week.

4. Recognize one team member publicly.

5. Model the behavior you expect.

CLOSING THOUGHT

"Leadership is not about being in charge. It is about taking care of those in your charge."

Choose to be more than a boss. Become a leader. Build a legacy.

PART V — ADVANCED LEADERSHIP INSIGHTS

A leader multiplies influence

CHAPTER 31 — Leadership and Emotional Intelligence

"People will forget what you said, people will forget what you did, but people will never forget how you made them feel." — Maya Angelou

Introduction

Leadership is not only about vision, strategy, and decision-making.
At its core, leadership is about people. And people are emotional beings.

The ability to understand, manage, and wisely respond to emotions — both your own and those of others — is what separates average leaders from exceptional ones. This ability is known as **Emotional Intelligence (EI)**.

In today's world, where collaboration, diversity, remote work, and rapid change dominate the workplace, emotional intelligence is no longer optional. It is essential.

This chapter explores what emotional intelligence is, why it matters in leadership, its key components, and how leaders can develop emotional intelligence to lead with wisdom, empathy, and lasting impact.

WHAT IS EMOTIONAL INTELLIGENCE-

Emotional Intelligence is the capacity to:

- Recognize your own emotions
- Understand what those emotions mean
- Manage your emotional responses
- Recognize emotions in others
- Respond appropriately to those emotions

In simple terms: **IQ may get you hired. EI gets you promoted.**

A leader with high emotional intelligence does not merely react.

They respond with awareness, wisdom, and control.

WHY EMOTIONAL INTELLIGENCE MATTERS IN LEADERSHIP

1. Builds Trust

People follow leaders they trust. Trust is built when leaders are emotionally consistent, empathetic, and respectful.

2. Improves Communication

Emotionally intelligent leaders listen beyond words. They hear tone, observe body language, and respond thoughtfully.

3. Strengthens Team Relationships

Teams thrive when members feel understood, valued, and safe.

4. Reduces Conflict

Leaders with EI defuse tension rather than escalating it.

5. Increases Motivation

People give their best to leaders who connect emotionally.

6. Enhances Decision-Making

Clear emotional awareness prevents impulsive or fear-driven decisions.

THE FIVE CORE COMPONENTS OF EMOTIONAL INTELLIGENCE

Psychologist Daniel Goleman identifies five key dimensions:

1. Self-Awareness

The ability to recognize your emotions as they occur.

Self-aware leaders:

- Understand their strengths and weaknesses
- Recognize emotional triggers
- Remain grounded under pressure

Without self-awareness, leadership becomes reactionary.

2. Self-Regulation

The ability to control emotional impulses.

Self-regulated leaders:

- Think before reacting
- Remain calm in crisis
- Respond instead of exploding
- Maintain professionalism under stress

Self-regulation builds credibility and stability.

3. Motivation

Emotionally intelligent leaders are driven by purpose more than position.

They:

- Pursue excellence
- Remain optimistic
- Persevere through setbacks
- Inspire intrinsic motivation in others

4. Empathy

Empathy is the ability to understand emotions in others. Empathetic leaders:

- Listen deeply
- Validate feelings
- Consider perspectives
- Create psychological safety

Empathy is the bridge between authority and connection.

5. Social Skills

The ability to manage relationships effectively.

Leaders with strong social skills:

- Communicate clearly
- Resolve conflict peacefully
- Influence without manipulation

- Build collaborative cultures

EMOTIONAL INTELLIGENCE IN ACTION

Crisis Leadership

High-EI leaders:

- Stay calm

- Communicate hope

- Reduce panic

- Provide steady direction

Team Motivation

High-EI leaders:

- Recognize effort

- Encourage progress

- Address discouragement early

Conflict Resolution

High-EI leaders:

- Listen first

- Seek understanding

- Guide peaceful solutions

DEVELOPING EMOTIONAL INTELLIGENCE AS A LEADER

Emotional intelligence is not fixed. It can be developed deliberately.

1. Practice Self-Reflection

- Review daily interactions

- Ask: "How did I respond-"

- Identify emotional triggers

2. Seek Honest Feedback

- Ask trusted colleagues

- Invite constructive insight

- Remain teachable

3. Improve Listening Skills

- Listen to understand, not to reply

- Observe body language

- Be fully present

4. Manage Stress Wisely

- Rest adequately

- Maintain work-life balance

- Pray, meditate, or journal

5. Choose Your Response

- Pause before reacting

- Respond intentionally

BIBLICAL LEADERSHIP INSIGHT

"Everyone should be quick to listen, slow to speak and slow to become angry." — James 1:19

This timeless wisdom captures emotional intelligence in action.

CONCLUSION

Leadership without emotional intelligence is mechanical. Leadership with emotional intelligence is transformational.

The emotionally intelligent leader:

- Understands self

- Connects with others

- Inspires loyalty

- Builds healthy cultures

- Leaves lasting impact

Understanding emotional intelligence now leads us to examine the role of ethics in leadership.

KEY TAKEAWAYS

- Emotional intelligence is essential for effective leadership

- Self-awareness is the foundation of EI

- Empathy builds trust and loyalty

- Self-regulation prevents destructive reactions

- Social skills strengthen collaboration

REFLECTION QUESTIONS

1. How do I typically respond under stress?

2. What emotional triggers affect my leadership?

3. Do my team members feel heard by me?

4. How well do I manage conflict emotionally?

5. What EI area do I need to strengthen most?

ACTION STEPS

1. Practice pausing before responding today.

2. Ask one person for honest emotional feedback.

3. Observe emotions in your next meeting.

4. Listen fully without interrupting.

5. Reflect nightly on emotional responses.

CLOSING THOUGHT

"A leader's greatest strength is not controlling others —
but mastering themselves."

Grow your emotional intelligence. And you will grow your
leadership influence

CHAPTER 32 — Ethics in Leadership

"A good name is more desirable than great riches; to be esteemed is better than silver or gold." — Proverbs 22:1

Introduction

Ethics in leadership is the foundation of trust, integrity, and credibility. Without ethics, leadership collapses into manipulation.
With ethics, leadership becomes a force for lasting impact.

Ethical leadership is not merely about obeying rules or avoiding wrongdoing. It is about consistently choosing what is right — even when it is difficult, costly, or unpopular. Leaders who prioritize ethics build organizations where trust flourishes, people feel safe, and long-term success becomes possible.

In an age where scandals, corruption, and broken trust have destroyed many great institutions, ethical leadership has never been more essential.

This chapter explores the importance of ethics in leadership, the core principles that guide ethical behavior, how to build an ethical culture, and how to navigate ethical dilemmas with wisdom and courage.

1. THE IMPORTANCE OF ETHICS IN LEADERSHIP

1.1 Building Trust and Credibility

Trust is the currency of leadership. Ethical behavior earns trust; unethical behavior destroys it.

When leaders act with honesty, fairness, and consistency,
people feel secure in following them. Trustworthy leaders
inspire loyalty, commitment, and discretionary effort —
the willingness of people to give more than what is
required.

Without trust, leadership becomes supervision.
With trust, leadership becomes influence.

1.2 Enhancing Organizational Reputation

An organization's reputation reflects its leadership's ethics.
Ethical leadership attracts:

- Top talent

- Loyal customers

- Strategic partners

- Investor confidence

Unethical leadership invites:

- Scandals

- Legal exposure

- Brand damage

- Loss of stakeholder confidence

Reputation takes years to build and seconds to destroy.
Ethical leaders guard it carefully.

1.3 Promoting a Positive Organizational Culture

Culture flows from leadership. Ethical leaders model honesty,
respect, fairness, and accountability — and these values
become embedded throughout the organization.

A strong ethical culture:

- Reduces internal conflict

- Increases engagement

- Encourages responsibility

- Strengthens teamwork

People mirror what leadership tolerates — or celebrates.

1.4 Ensuring Compliance and Avoiding Legal Risk

Ethical leadership naturally promotes compliance with laws and regulations. Instead of reacting to legal problems, ethical leaders prevent them by:

- Establishing clear standards

- Training employees

- Encouraging transparency

- Acting promptly when issues arise

Prevention is always cheaper than damage control.

2. CORE PRINCIPLES OF ETHICAL LEADERSHIP

2.1 Integrity

Integrity means doing the right thing when no one is watching.

Leaders with integrity:

- Keep their word
- Align actions with values
- Reject shortcuts that compromise character
- Stand for truth over convenience

Integrity is the backbone of credibility.

2.2 Accountability

Ethical leaders take responsibility for outcomes — good or bad.

They:

- Admit mistakes
- Learn from failure
- Avoid blame-shifting
- Hold themselves and others responsible

Accountability builds maturity and trust.

2.3 Fairness

Fairness means impartiality, justice, and consistency.

Ethical leaders:

- Avoid favoritism

- Base decisions on merit

- Treat people with dignity

- Provide equal opportunity

Fairness creates unity and respect.

2.4 Respect for Others

Respect acknowledges the value of every person.

Ethical leaders:

- Listen actively

- Welcome diverse views

- Communicate courteously

- Honor human dignity

Respect breeds loyalty.

2.5 Transparency

Transparency means openness in communication and decision-making.

Ethical leaders:

- Share information honestly

- Explain reasoning behind decisions

- Invite feedback

- Avoid hidden agendas

Transparency eliminates suspicion and builds confidence.

3. CULTIVATING AN ETHICAL CULTURE

3.1 Leading by Example

Ethical leadership starts at the top. People may ignore speeches, but they always watch behavior.

Leaders who live the values they teach establish credibility and inspire imitation.

3.2 Establishing Clear Ethical Standards

Ethical cultures are built intentionally.

Leaders should:

- Create a code of ethics
- Define acceptable behaviors
- Provide ethics training
- Reinforce expectations regularly

Clarity prevents confusion.

3.3 Encouraging Open Communication

Ethical leaders create safe environments where people can speak up without fear.

They:

- Welcome concerns
- Protect whistleblowers
- Listen without retaliation
- Act on reported issues

Silence breeds corruption. Openness prevents it.

3.4 Recognizing Ethical Behavior

What gets rewarded gets repeated.

Ethical leaders:

- Celebrate honesty

- Praise integrity

- Promote value-driven employees

Recognition reinforces culture.

3.5 Addressing Unethical Behavior Promptly

Unaddressed misconduct spreads.

Ethical leaders:

- Investigate thoroughly

- Apply fair discipline

- Communicate outcomes appropriately

- Restore trust through action

Consistency protects integrity.

4. NAVIGATING ETHICAL DILEMMAS

4.1 Understanding Ethical Dilemmas

Ethical dilemmas occur when:

- Values conflict

- Interests collide

- Consequences are unclear

Leaders must decide not only what is profitable — but what is right.

4.2 Applying Ethical Decision Models

Wise ethical decision-making asks:

- Is it legal?

- Is it fair?

- Is it transparent?

- Would I be proud if it were publicized?

- Does it align with our values?

If any answer is no — reconsider.

4.3 Seeking Counsel

Ethical leaders do not walk alone.

They consult:

- Trusted advisors

- Mentors

- Boards

- Spiritual guidance

Wisdom multiplies through counsel.

4.4 Reflecting on Outcomes

After decisions, ethical leaders reflect:

- What did I learn?

- Did this strengthen trust?

- What can improve next time?

Reflection sharpens moral judgment.

BIBLICAL LEADERSHIP INSIGHT

"Whoever walks in integrity walks securely,
    but whoever takes crooked paths will be found out."
    — Proverbs 10:9

Ethical leadership is ultimately leadership that can stand in
the light.

CONCLUSION

Ethics is not an accessory to leadership — it is its foundation.

Without ethics:

- Trust collapses

- Culture decays

- Reputation erodes

- Leadership fails

With ethics:

- Trust deepens

- Culture strengthens

- Legacy endures

True leadership is measured not only by results achieved, but
by character displayed along the way.

Ethical leaders build organizations that succeed — and souls
that remain whole. With ethical foundations established,
we now explore the concept of total leadership and
holistic influence.

KEY TAKEAWAYS

- Ethics is the foundation of credible leadership

- Integrity earns lasting trust

- Culture reflects leadership behavior

- Transparency builds confidence

- Ethical courage protects long-term success

REFLECTION QUESTIONS

- Do my actions match my stated values-

- How do I handle mistakes — mine and others-

- Would I be comfortable if my decisions were public-

- Do people feel safe speaking truth to me-

- What ethical standard do I need to strengthen most-

ACTION STEPS

1. Review your personal leadership values.

2. Write a personal code of ethics.

3. Ask a trusted colleague how ethically consistent you appear.

4. Commit to one ethical improvement this week.

5. Reward ethical behavior you observe in others.

CLOSING THOUGHT

"Character is doing the right thing when nobody's looking."
— J. C. Watts Build your leadership on ethics.
And your leadership will outlive your position.

CHAPTER 33 — Total Leadership

"He who rules his spirit is greater than he who takes a city."
— Proverbs 16:32

Introduction — Understanding Total Leadership

Leadership is not something we switch on at work and switch off at home. True leadership is whole-life leadership.

Total Leadership is the ability to lead effectively across every major dimension of life — professional, personal, social, and spiritual. It recognizes that a leader is not only a CEO in the office, but a spouse at home, a parent in the family, a citizen in the community, and a steward of their own soul.

Many leaders succeed professionally but fail personally. Others grow spiritually but neglect professional excellence.
Total Leadership harmonizes all domains, creating a life of balance, integrity, and sustained impact.

It is leadership without compartments.

1. THE FOUR DOMAINS OF TOTAL LEADERSHIP

Total Leadership rests on four interconnected domains:

1.1 Work / Professional Leadership

This is leadership in your career, business, or organizational role.

It involves:

- Casting vision

- Driving performance

- Developing people

- Achieving results

- Modeling excellence

But Total Leadership insists that professional success must align with personal values — not replace them.

1.2 Family / Personal Leadership

Leadership begins at home.

This domain includes:

- Being a present spouse

- A nurturing parent

- A faithful friend

- A responsible household leader

A leader who cannot lead at home cannot sustain credibility elsewhere.
Family is the first leadership laboratory.

1.3 Community / Social Leadership

Total leaders serve beyond themselves.

This domain involves:

- Contributing to community welfare

- Serving causes larger than self

- Mentoring others

- Building social impact

Legacy is measured not only by profit — but by people lifted.

1.4 Self/Spiritual Leadership

At the center of Total Leadership is self-leadership.

This includes:

- Self-awareness
- Character formation
- Emotional mastery
- Spiritual grounding
- Purpose clarity

A leader who cannot lead himself cannot lead others effectively.

Self-leadership is the root of all other leadership.

2. INTEGRATION OF THE FOUR DOMAINS

Traditional leadership separates life into compartments.
Total Leadership integrates them.

2.1 Work–Life Balance

Total leaders align professional ambition with:

- Family priorities

- Health

- Faith

- Personal growth

Balance is not dividing time equally —
It is aligning life intentionally.

2.2 Synergy Across Domains

Skills learned in one domain strengthen another:

- Professional communication improves family connection

- Spiritual discipline strengthens workplace integrity

- Community service deepens empathy in leadership

- Parenting refines patience in management

Everything becomes connected.

3. BENEFITS OF TOTAL LEADERSHIP

3.1 Enhanced Well-Being

- Reduced stress

- Greater emotional stability

- Prevention of burnout

- Increased life satisfaction

Whole leaders live healthier lives.

3.2 Increased Leadership Effectiveness

- Authentic presence

- Emotional intelligence

- Stronger influence

- Higher credibility

People follow whole leaders naturally.

3.3 Stronger Relationships

- Deeper family bonds

- Trust-filled teams

- Loyal partnerships

- Meaningful friendships

Relationships are the true reward of leadership.

3.4 Sustainable Success

Many leaders rise fast and fall hard.
Total leaders rise steadily and remain strong — because no domain is neglected.

4. IMPLEMENTING TOTAL LEADERSHIP

4.1 Self-Assessment

Ask yourself:

- How am I leading at work?

- How am I leading at home?

- How am I serving my community?

- How am I leading myself?

Awareness precedes growth.

4.2 Set Domain Goals

Set intentional goals for:

- Career

- Family

- Community

- Personal growth

Alignment prevents regret.

4.3 Integrate Domains

- Involve family in community service

- Bring personal growth into professional practice

- Let faith guide ethical decisions

- Let work skills bless society

Live one life — not four disconnected lives.

4.4 Continuous Improvement

Total Leadership is a journey, not a destination.

Review regularly:

- What is improving?

- What needs adjustment?

- What must I realign?

Growth keeps leadership fresh.

BIBLICAL LEADERSHIP INSIGHT

"Teach us to number our days,
   that we may gain a heart of wisdom." — Psalm 90:12

Wise leaders steward every domain intentionally.

CONCLUSION — THE PATH TO HOLISTIC LEADERSHIP

Total Leadership is leadership with wholeness.

It is:

- Professional excellence
- Family faithfulness
- Community service
- Personal integrity

When these align, leadership becomes legacy.

A leader who conquers boardrooms but loses family has failed.
A leader who grows wealth but loses soul has failed.
A leader who balances all domains has achieved true success.

Total Leadership builds leaders whose lives preach louder than their words. Understanding total leadership now prepares us to examine the key dimensions — the arms of leadership.

KEY TAKEAWAYS

- Leadership is whole-life, not workplace only

- Self-leadership is the foundation of all leadership

- Balance produces sustainability

- Integration multiplies impact

- Legacy is built across all domains

REFLECTION QUESTIONS

1. Which domain of my life is strongest right now?

2. Which domain am I neglecting?

3. Do my professional goals align with my personal values?

4. How am I leading at home?

5. What legacy am I building across all four domains?

ACTION STEPS

1. Rate yourself 1–10 in each domain.

2. Write one improvement goal for each.

3. Schedule weekly reflection time.

4. Align next month's calendar with your domain goals.

5. Ask a trusted person for honest feedback.

CLOSING THOUGHT

"Success without fulfillment is the greatest failure."

Lead totally. Live wholly. Leave a legacy that touches every sphere of life.

CHAPTER 34 — The Arms of Leadership

"Leadership is practiced not in isolation, but in every sphere where people gather, grow, and govern."

Introduction

Leadership is not limited to boardrooms or pulpits. It extends into every sector of society where influence is required, people are guided, and futures are shaped.

These spheres are the **Arms of Leadership** — the domains where leadership principles take on specialized forms depending on context, responsibility, and impact.

Understanding these arms equips a leader to recognize:

- Where they are called to lead

- How leadership must adapt by domain

- Why no sphere thrives without strong leadership

This chapter explores the major arms of leadership and their distinct functions in shaping civilization.

1. POLITICAL LEADERSHIP

Definition:
Political leadership involves guiding nations, governments, and public institutions through governance, lawmaking, and public service.

Core Functions:

- Establishing policies and laws

- Representing citizens' interests

- Managing national resources
- Navigating diplomacy and global relations
- Protecting justice and civil order

Legacy Example: Nelson Mandela — whose leadership dismantled apartheid and united South Africa through reconciliation and moral authority.

Leadership Insight: Political leadership determines the destiny of nations.

2. EDUCATIONAL LEADERSHIP

Definition:

Educational leadership guides schools, universities, and training institutions toward academic excellence and character formation.

Core Functions:

- Designing curriculum
- Developing teachers and faculty
- Creating environments for learning
- Shaping future generations
- Building knowledge-driven societies

Legacy Example:

Maria Montessori — whose child-centered educational model revolutionized global learning systems.

Leadership Insight:

Education leadership builds tomorrow's leaders.

3. BUSINESS LEADERSHIP

Definition:
Business leadership steers organizations toward innovation, profitability, sustainability, and market relevance.

Core Functions:

- Strategic planning
- Financial stewardship
- Innovation and growth
- Team development
- Market expansion

Legacy Example:
Steve Jobs — who transformed technology and consumer culture through visionary innovation.

Leadership Insight:
Business leadership fuels economic progress.

4. RELIGIOUS LEADERSHIP

Definition:
Religious leadership guides faith communities through spiritual instruction, moral direction, and service to humanity.

Core Functions:

- Teaching spiritual truth
- Shepherding communities
- Moral and ethical guidance
- Counseling and discipleship
- Social compassion initiatives

Legacy Example:
Pope Francis — whose leadership emphasizes humility, compassion, and service to the marginalized.

Leadership Insight:
Religious leadership shapes conscience and character.

5. HEALTHCARE LEADERSHIP

Definition:
Healthcare leadership directs hospitals, clinics, and public health systems to provide quality care and medical advancement.

Core Functions:

- Ensuring patient care excellence
- Managing health systems
- Leading crisis response
- Promoting public health policies
- Supporting medical innovation

Legacy Example:
Dr. Anthony Fauci — whose leadership guided global pandemic response efforts.

Leadership Insight:
Healthcare leadership preserves life.

6. MILITARY LEADERSHIP

Definition:
Military leadership involves commanding armed forces in defense of national security and peacekeeping missions.

Core Functions:

- Strategic defense planning

- Tactical execution

- Discipline and order

- Ethical conduct in conflict

- Protection of national sovereignty

Legacy Example:
General Dwight D. Eisenhower — Supreme Allied Commander in World War II.

Leadership Insight:
Military leadership safeguards freedom.

7. SOCIAL LEADERSHIP

Definition:
Social leadership drives community development, advocacy, and justice-centered movements.

Core Functions:

- Mobilizing communities

- Advocating for equality

- Leading social reforms

- Empowering marginalized groups

- Creating grassroots change

Legacy Example:
Dr. Martin Luther King Jr. — whose leadership advanced civil rights and justice.

Leadership Insight:
Social leadership heals society.

8. CULTURAL LEADERSHIP

Definition:
Cultural leadership preserves heritage, promotes identity, and advances artistic expression.

Core Functions:

- Protecting cultural heritage
- Encouraging creative arts
- Strengthening national identity
- Unifying diverse populations
- Storytelling and tradition-keeping

Legacy Example:
Otumfuo Osei Tutu II — whose cultural leadership preserves Ashanti heritage while advancing modern development.

Leadership Insight:
Cultural leadership sustains identity.

INTEGRATED INSIGHT — THE INTERCONNECTED ARMS

No arm of leadership operates in isolation.

- Political decisions influence education
- Education fuels business innovation
- Business funds healthcare systems
- Religion shapes ethics
- Culture strengthens unity
- Social leadership drives justice

- Military leadership protects peace

CONCLUSION

Leadership is multidimensional. Strength, wisdom, influence, and character must work together to create balance and effectiveness. When these elements are aligned, leadership becomes both powerful and sustainable.

With these dimensions in mind, we now explore the key factors that influence leadership effectiveness.

KEY TAKEAWAYS

- Leadership exists in every societal domain
- Each arm requires specialized leadership skills
- Every arm contributes to national and global progress
- Effective leaders understand their sphere of influence
- Integrated leadership builds lasting civilization

REFLECTION QUESTIONS

1. Which arm of leadership am I currently operating in?

2. Which arm am I called to influence next?

3. How does my leadership contribute to society's progress?

4. Which arm most needs ethical leadership today?

5. What legacy will my leadership leave in my chosen domain?

ACTION STEPS

1. Identify your primary leadership domain.

2. Study great leaders in that arm.

3. Develop skills unique to that sphere.

4. Build partnerships across other arms.

5. Commit to serving beyond personal success.

CLOSING THOUGHT

A true legacy leader does not merely lead in one arena — thy understand how every arm of leadership shapes humanity's future.

Find your arm. Master your assignment. Serve your generation.

CHAPTER 35 — Four Factors That Influence Leadership

"Leadership success is never accidental. It is the result of understanding people, mastering communication, reading situations wisely, and leading yourself well."

Introduction

Leadership is not performed in isolation. Every leadership experience is shaped by four powerful and interconnected factors:

1. **The Leader**
2. **The Followers**
3. **Communication**
4. **The Situation**

When these four elements are understood and mastered, leadership becomes effective, adaptive, and enduring. When they are ignored, leadership becomes frustrating, inconsistent, and ineffective.

This chapter explores how each factor influences leadership success and how legacy leaders learn to master them.

1. THE LEADER

Leadership begins with the leader. Before leading others, one must learn to lead oneself.

1.1 Self-Awareness and Authenticity

Effective leadership starts with knowing:

- Who you are
  - What you believe
  - What you value
  - What you can do
  - Where you must grow

Self-aware leaders lead authentically. They do not pretend, perform, or manipulate. Authenticity builds credibility, trust, and emotional connection with followers.

People follow leaders who are real.

1.2 Building Trust

John C. Maxwell rightly said: **"Trust is the foundation of leadership."**

Without trust:

- Influence disappears
  - Motivation declines
  - Loyalty fades
  - Vision stalls

Trust is built through:

- Consistency
  - Transparency
  - Integrity
  - Keeping promises
  - Owning mistakes

Legacy leaders understand:

You cannot lead people who do not trust you.

1.3 Continuous Learning and Growth

Leadership is not a destination — it is a journey.

Great leaders:

- Read consistently
- Learn continuously
- Seek mentorship
- Reflect regularly
- Remain teachable

When leaders grow, followers grow.
When leaders stop learning, leadership stops progressing.

2. THE FOLLOWERS

Leadership does not exist without followers. Understanding people is the heart of leadership.

2.1 Understanding Your Team

Every follower is different:

- Different motivations
- Different abilities
- Different personalities
- Different experiences

Effective leaders take time to understand:

- What drives each person
- What support they need
- How they best contribute

One-size leadership never fits all.

2.2 Adapting Leadership Styles

A wise leader adjusts leadership style according to follower needs:

- New team members need guidance
- Skilled team members need empowerment
- Struggling team members need coaching
- High performers need trust

Flexibility is a hallmark of mature leadership.

2.3 Empowering and Motivating

Followers thrive when leaders:

- Provide resources
- Create opportunity
- Recognize effort
- Celebrate progress
- Give ownership

Empowered followers become:

- Confident
- Creative
- Committed
- Productive

Great leaders do not create dependence — they create capacity.

3. COMMUNICATION

Communication is the bloodstream of leadership. Without communication, vision dies.

3.1 Two-Way Communication

Effective leadership communication includes:

- Speaking clearly
- Listening actively
- Asking thoughtful questions
- Encouraging honest feedback

Two-way communication builds:

- Alignment
- Engagement
- Trust
- Clarity

Leaders who only speak but never listen soon lose followers.

3.2 Nonverbal Communication and Leading by Example

Followers watch more than they hear.

- Actions speak louder than words
- Attitudes communicate silently
- Behavior sets standards

Leading by example is the most powerful leadership language.

People do what leaders do — not what they say.

3.3 Building Relationships

Strong communication builds:

- Strong relationships

- Emotional connection

- Team cohesion

- Psychological safety

People follow leaders they feel connected to.

4. THE SITUATION

Leadership is situational. What works today may not work tomorrow.

4.1 Adapting to Different Situations

Situations change:

- Crises

- Growth seasons

- Conflict moments

- Transition periods

- Opportunity windows

Effective leaders read situations quickly and respond wisely.

4.2 Timing and Context

Leadership effectiveness often depends on:

- When to act

- How to respond

- What tone to use

- Who to involve

Timing separates good leaders from great ones.

4.3 Situational Forces

Leaders operate within:

- Organizational culture
- Structural limitations
- Senior leadership expectations
- Team dynamics
- External pressures

Wise leaders understand these forces and navigate them strategically.

INTEGRATED INSIGHT

These four factors constantly interact:

- A growing leader builds strong followers
- Clear communication strengthens trust
- Understanding situations refines decisions
- Empowered followers improve outcomes

When all four align — leadership thrives.

CONCLUSION

Leadership is shaped by both internal and external forces. Awareness of these factors empowers leaders to navigate challenges, leverage opportunities, and maximize their effectiveness. Great leaders understand that influence is not accidental — it is cultivated.

With these influencing factors understood, we now turn to the importance of continuous learning and improvement in leadership.

KEY TAKEAWAYS

- Leadership begins with self-leadership

- Followers determine leadership effectiveness

- Communication sustains influence

- Situational awareness guides wisdom

- Mastering all four creates legacy leadership

REFLECTION QUESTIONS

1. How self-aware am I as a leader?

2. Do my followers feel understood and empowered?

3. How effective is my communication?

4. Do I read situations accurately?

5. Which factor do I need to strengthen most?

CLOSING THOUGHT

Leadership excellence is never accidental.
It is the daily mastery of:

The Leader.
The Followers.

The Communication.
The Situation.

Master these —
   and you master leadership itself.

CHAPTER 36 — Continuous Learning and Improvement for Leadership

"The moment a leader stops learning is the moment leadership begins to decline."

Introduction

Leadership is not a destination — it is a lifelong journey of growth.
In a world that evolves daily through technology, globalization, and social transformation, leaders who stop learning quickly become outdated. Continuous learning and improvement are therefore not optional for leaders — they are essential.

Legacy leaders understand that relevance is sustained only through renewal. They commit themselves to learning, adapting, and evolving so they can continue to inspire, guide, and influence effectively.

This chapter explores the necessity of continuous learning, the mindset required to sustain it, and the transformational impact it has on leadership excellence.

1. THE IMPERATIVE OF CONTINUOUS LEARNING

Continuous learning is the intentional pursuit of knowledge, skill, and wisdom for personal and professional advancement.

1.1 Staying Relevant in a Changing World

Change is relentless.

- New technologies emerge

- Industries evolve

- Workforce expectations shift

- Global realities transform

Leaders who do not learn fall behind.
Leaders who learn continuously stay ahead.

Continuous learning equips leaders to:

- Understand emerging trends

- Adapt to disruption

- Anticipate opportunity

- Navigate uncertainty confidently

1.2 Enhancing Leadership Competence

Leadership effectiveness expands through exposure.

Learning enables leaders to:

- Strengthen existing abilities

- Acquire new skills

- Improve emotional intelligence

- Broaden strategic thinking

- Refine decision-making

Leadership mastery is built over time — never assumed at once.

1.3 Fostering a Culture of Innovation

Leaders who learn create learning organizations.

Their curiosity spreads:

- Creativity increases

- Experimentation becomes safe

- Innovation flourishes

- Continuous improvement becomes cultural

When leaders model learning, followers follow.

2. CULTIVATING A LEARNING MINDSET

Continuous learning begins with mindset — not opportunity.

2.1 Embracing Curiosity

Curiosity is the engine of growth.

Legacy leaders:

- Ask questions

- Explore new ideas

- Seek understanding

- Challenge assumptions

Curious leaders discover what others overlook.

2.2 Overcoming Fear of Failure

Failure is not the opposite of success — it is part of it.

Learning leaders:

- Treat mistakes as lessons

- Extract wisdom from setbacks

- Develop resilience

- Encourage intelligent risk-taking

- Fear shrinks leadership.

- Learning expands leadership.

2.3 Seeking and Valuing Feedback

Feedback is a mirror for growth.

Effective leaders:

- Invite honest input
- Listen without defensiveness
- Apply insight wisely
- Appreciate correction

Feedback-refined leaders grow faster than self-satisfied leaders.

3. STRATEGIES FOR CONTINUOUS IMPROVEMENT

Learning must be intentional — not accidental.

3.1 Setting Personal Development Goals

Legacy Leaders set growth targets:

- New competencies
- Knowledge areas
- Leadership qualities
- Character refinement

What gets scheduled gets developed.

3.2 Engaging in Lifelong Learning

Continuous learning avenues include:

- Books and study

- Courses and seminars

- Coaching and mentorship

- Conferences and networks

- Podcasts and research

Leaders who read lead.

Leaders who learn last.

3.3 Reflection and Self-Assessment

Growth requires reflection.

Wise leaders ask:

- What did I learn today?

- What could I improve?

- What must I change?

Reflection converts experience into wisdom.

4. THE IMPACT OF CONTINUOUS LEARNING ON LEADERSHIP

4.1 Building Credibility and Trust

Followers trust leaders who grow.

A learning leader:

- Models humility

- Demonstrates discipline

- Earns respect

- Inspires imitation

4.2 Enhancing Decision-Making

Learning broadens perspective.

Informed leaders:

- See options clearly
- Weigh consequences wisely
- Decide strategically
- Avoid narrow thinking

4.3 Driving Organizational Success

Organizations rise to the learning level of their leaders.

Continuous-learning leaders:

- Innovate consistently
- Adapt rapidly
- Remain competitive
- Build resilient teams

5. OVERCOMING BARRIERS TO CONTINUOUS LEARNING

5.1 Time Constraints

Legacy leaders:

- Schedule learning time
- Protect growth habits
- Treat development as priority

If growth isn't scheduled, it won't happen.

5.2 Information Overload

Wise leaders:

- Filter sources
- Choose relevance

- Focus on depth over noise

5.3 Complacency

Complacency is leadership decay.

Growth-minded leaders:

- Challenge comfort zones

- Set new goals

- Pursue higher levels

- Refuse stagnation

CONCLUSION

Continuous learning is the lifeline of effective leadership. Leaders who commit to growth remain relevant, adaptable, and impactful in an ever-changing world. Learning sharpens competence, strengthens character, and expands perspective — enabling leaders to guide others with clarity and confidence.

The difference between declining leadership and enduring leadership is the commitment to improvement. Those who stop learning begin to lose influence; those who keep learning continue to lead with strength and vision.

Ultimately, leadership excellence is not achieved in a moment — it is built over time through intentional growth, reflection, and renewal. Leaders who embrace continuous learning do not just keep up with change — they lead it.

With this foundation of continuous growth, we now turn

to leadership development and the intentional process of building leaders for today and tomorrow.

KEY TAKEAWAYS

- Learning keeps leaders relevant
- Curiosity fuels innovation
- Feedback accelerates growth
- Reflection converts experience into wisdom
- Continuous learning builds legacy

REFLECTION QUESTIONS

1. What am I currently learning as a leader?

2. How often do I seek feedback?

3. What growth goal will I pursue this year?

4. Where have I become complacent?

5. What daily habit will strengthen my leadership learning?

CLOSING THOUGHT

Leadership excellence is not achieved once — it is renewed daily.

Leaders who stop learning stop leading.
Leaders who keep learning keep rising.

May your leadership journey remain one of continuous growth, expanding influence, and enduring legacy.

CHAPTER 37 — Leadership Development: Building Leaders for Today and Tomorrow

Introduction

Leadership development is the ongoing process of enhancing an individual's ability to influence, guide, and inspire others effectively. It involves cultivating the skills, behaviors, mindset, and character necessary to lead in an ever-changing world. In today's dynamic environment — where organizations face continuous shifts in technology, culture, and market demands — the importance of leadership development cannot be overstated.

Great leaders are not accidental; they are intentionally formed. Leadership development ensures that individuals grow from merely holding positions of authority into becoming transformational leaders who empower others, drive innovation, and sustain long-term success. It is not a one-time event but a lifelong commitment to growth, refinement, and excellence.

1. THE IMPORTANCE OF LEADERSHIP DEVELOPMENT

Leadership development is crucial for both individuals and organizations because it builds the foundation for sustainable progress and resilience.

1. Sustaining Organizational Growth

Every thriving organization requires capable leaders who can adapt to change, solve complex problems, and chart strategic direction. Leadership development creates a pipeline of prepared leaders ready to step into greater responsibilities and guide the organization forward.

2. Enhancing Employee Engagement

Effective leaders inspire commitment, motivation, and loyalty. When leaders are well-developed, they create environments where people feel valued, heard, and empowered. Engaged employees are more productive, innovative, and dedicated to organizational success.

3. Fostering Innovation

Leadership development encourages strategic thinking, creativity, and openness to new ideas. Leaders trained to think beyond routine operations stimulate innovation and continuous improvement across teams.

4. Building Resilience

Challenges, crises, and uncertainty are inevitable. Developed leaders possess emotional strength, adaptability, and composure, enabling them to guide teams confidently through adversity.

5. Ensuring Leadership Continuity

Succession planning depends on leadership development. Organizations that intentionally develop leaders avoid disruption when transitions occur and maintain stability through generations of leadership.

2. KEY COMPONENTS OF LEADERSHIP DEVELOPMENT

Leadership development is multi-dimensional. It strengthens both inner character and outward competence.

1. Self-Awareness

Self-awareness is the foundation of leadership growth.
Leaders must understand their strengths, weaknesses,
values, motives, and impact on others. Through reflection
and feedback, leaders gain clarity about who they are and
how they lead.

2. Skill Development

Leadership requires practical competencies —
communication, decision-making, conflict resolution,
team-building, and strategic planning. These skills are
sharpened through training, experience, and deliberate
practice.

3. Emotional Intelligence

Effective leaders understand both their emotions and those
of others. Emotional intelligence allows leaders to
manage stress, resolve conflict, build trust, and cultivate
strong relationships.

4. Mentorship and Coaching

Mentors and coaches accelerate leadership growth by offering
guidance, accountability, wisdom, and perspective. Great
leaders are often shaped by those who have walked ahead
of them.

5. Strategic Thinking

Leaders must see beyond present circumstances and
anticipate future trends. Strategic thinking enables leaders
to align daily actions with long-term vision.

6. Adaptability and Change Leadership

Leadership development equips individuals to embrace change rather than fear it. Adaptable leaders navigate uncertainty, adjust strategies, and help teams transition smoothly.

7. Ethical and Values-Based Leadership

Leadership without integrity is dangerous. Leadership development must strengthen moral courage, accountability, and ethical decision-making.

8. Communication Excellence

Leaders succeed or fail by communication. Leadership development refines the ability to speak clearly, listen actively, persuade effectively, and inspire confidently.

3. THE LAW OF PROCESS — LEADERSHIP IS DEVELOPED DAILY

Leadership expert John C. Maxwell states:

"Leadership is developed daily, not in a day."

This principle, known as the **Law of Process**, reminds us that leadership growth happens through consistent daily habits, not sudden breakthroughs. Just as physical fitness requires regular exercise, leadership strength comes from regular discipline — reading, reflecting, practicing, learning, and applying.

Small daily improvements compound into extraordinary leadership capacity over time.

4. THE FIVE STAGES OF LEADERSHIP GROWTH

Leadership growth follows recognizable stages:

Stage 1: I Don't Know What I Don't Know

At this stage, individuals are unaware of the importance of leadership. They miss opportunities simply because they do not recognize leadership's value.

Stage 2: I Know That I Need to Know

Here, individuals recognize leadership's importance, often after stepping into responsibility and realizing the need for guidance.

Stage 3: I Know What I Don't Know

Awareness deepens. Leaders identify gaps in their skills and intentionally pursue growth.

Stage 4: I Know and Grow — It Starts to Show

Learning becomes visible in behavior. Influence increases. Confidence rises. Results improve.

Stage 5: I Simply Go Because of What I Know

Leadership becomes natural. Principles are internalized. The leader now multiplies other leaders.

5. PERSONAL LEADERSHIP DEVELOPMENT — DAILY PRACTICE

Personal leadership development requires intentional habits:

- Reading leadership books
- Attending seminars and workshops
- Seeking mentorship
- Practicing reflection
- Receiving feedback
- Taking on new challenges• Serving others

Leadership growth is self-driven. No one grows accidentally.

6. OVERCOMING BARRIERS TO LEADERSHIP DEVELOPMENT

Time Constraints

Leaders must schedule growth like any other priority.

Complacency

Comfort is the enemy of growth. Great leaders remain students forever.

Fear of Failure

Failure is a teacher. Leaders grow by trying, learning, and improving.

Lack of Accountability

Accountable environments accelerate leadership maturity.

CONCLUSION

Leadership development is the engine that drives personal transformation and organizational excellence. It shapes ordinary individuals into extraordinary influencers, visionaries, and builders of legacy. Leaders who commit to continuous growth gain the wisdom to lead wisely, the courage to lead boldly, and the humility to lead faithfully.

Leadership is not a destination — it is a daily journey. Understanding leadership development now leads us to explore the relationship between leadership and management.

KEY TAKEAWAYS

- Leadership development is continuous
- Growth happens daily, not instantly
- Self-awareness is the starting point
- Emotional intelligence strengthens leadership
- Integrity sustains influence
- Leaders who grow themselves grow others

REFLECTION QUESTIONS

1. What am I doing daily to develop my leadership capacity?

2. Which leadership skill do I need to strengthen most?

3. Who is mentoring or coaching my growth?

4. How do I respond to feedback?

5. What leadership habit will I commit to this month?

ACTION STEPS

1. Commit to daily leadership reading

2. Seek honest feedback monthly

3. Join a leadership community

4. Practice leading new initiatives

5. Keep a leadership development journal

Closing Thought

Leadership greatness is not gifted — it is grown. Those who grow daily will lead powerfully tomorrow.

CHAPTER 38 — Leadership vs. Management: Vision, Execution, and Balanced Influence

Introduction

In the landscapes of business, ministry, government, and organizational development, the terms *leadership* and *management* are often used interchangeably. Yet while both are essential to success, they represent distinct roles with unique responsibilities.

Organizations rarely fail because they lack vision or systems. They fail because they misunderstand the balance between leadership and management.

Leadership provides direction. Management provides structure. Leadership inspires movement. Management sustains momentum.

Understanding the difference between leadership and management is crucial for anyone aspiring to excel in either — or both. This chapter explores their distinctions, their complementary nature, and how organizations can cultivate strong leaders and skilled managers to achieve sustainable success.

DEFINING LEADERSHIP AND MANAGEMENT

Leadership

Leadership is the art of inspiring, motivating, and guiding individuals or teams toward a shared vision or purpose. Leaders are visionaries who influence others to realize their potential and pursue meaningful objectives.

Leadership is associated with innovation, emotional intelligence, courage, and the ability to mobilize people toward change.

A leader asks: **"Where are we going — and why?"**

Management

Management is the process of planning, organizing, directing, and controlling resources — including people, finances, time, and information — to achieve specific objectives efficiently. Managers ensure stability, consistency, accountability, and operational excellence.

A manager asks: **"How will we get there — and when?"**

Leadership without management creates chaos. Management without leadership creates stagnation.

Both are necessary. Both are powerful. Together, they produce excellence.

KEY DIFFERENCES BETWEEN LEADERS AND MANAGERS

1. Vision vs. Execution

Leaders create and communicate vision for the future. They challenge the status quo and inspire people toward new possibilities.

Managers translate vision into action. They execute plans, align daily operations, and ensure objectives are achieved.

2. Inspiration vs. Control

Leaders inspire trust, passion, and commitment. They connect emotionally and lead by example.

Managers maintain control through systems, supervision, policies, and performance monitoring.

3. People vs. Processes

Leaders prioritize people — developing, empowering, and nurturing talent.

Managers prioritize processes — optimizing systems, workflows, and efficiency.

4. Change vs. Stability

Leaders are agents of change. They embrace uncertainty and drive innovation. Managers are guardians of stability. They minimize risk and maintain order.

5. Long-Term vs. Short-Term Focus

Leaders focus on long-term purpose, destiny, and strategic direction. Managers focus on short-term execution, targets, and deadlines.

THE COMPLEMENTARY ROLES OF LEADERS AND MANAGERS

Great organizations do not choose between leadership and management — they integrate both.

- Leaders define the destination; managers design the roadmap.

- Leaders ignite passion; managers build discipline.

- Leaders grow people; managers improve performance.

- Leader's champion change; managers implement change.

- Leaders think strategically; managers execute tactically.

When leadership and management operate in harmony, organizations flourish.

DEVELOPING BOTH LEADERSHIP AND MANAGEMENT SKILLS

Becoming a complete organizational contributor requires developing both capacities.

1. Self-Awareness

Understand your natural inclination. Are you more visionary or more structured- Awareness enables balanced growth.

2. Continuous Learning

Engage in leadership and management development — strategy, communication, emotional intelligence, project management, and decision-making.

3. Practical Experience

Lead teams. Manage projects. Rotate responsibilities. Experience sharpens competence.

4. Mentorship and Coaching

Learn from visionary leaders and operational managers. Both perspectives refine your effectiveness.

5. Feedback and Reflection

Consistent feedback strengthens leadership presence and managerial precision.

BALANCING LEADERSHIP AND MANAGEMENT IN ORGANIZATIONS

1. Encourage Collaboration

Promote unity between visionary leaders and operational managers.

2. Provide Development Pathways

Train future leaders in management skills and managers in leadership capacity.

3. Recognize Both Contributions

Celebrate visionary breakthroughs and operational excellence equally.

4. Align With Organizational Mission

Ensuring leadership and management both serve the organization's purpose.

5. Foster a Culture of Balance

Value innovation and discipline, inspiration and accountability, people and performance.

ILLUSTRATIVE CONTRASTS

- The manager administers; the leader innovates.
- The manager maintains; the leader develops.
- The manager focuses on systems; the leader focuses on people.
- The manager controls; the leader inspires trust.

- The manager asks how and when; the leader asks what and why.

- The manager watches today; the leader prepares tomorrow.

- The manager does things right; the leader does the right thing.

CONCLUSION

Leadership sets direction. Management ensures delivery. Organizations that cultivate only leadership risk instability. Organizations that cultivate only management risk stagnation.

But organizations that integrate both build enduring excellence. For individuals, mastering both leadership and management creates rare effectiveness — the ability to envision boldly, plan wisely, execute faithfully, and inspire consistently. With this distinction clarified, we now examine the qualifications and criteria for selecting great leaders.

KEY TAKEAWAYS

- Leadership and management are distinct but inseparable.

- Leadership provides vision; management provides structure.

- Leaders inspire movement; managers sustain momentum.

- Great organizations cultivate both strong leaders and strong managers.

- Individuals who master both become highly effective agents of change.

REFLECTION QUESTIONS

1. In your current role, do you function more as a leader or as a manager?

2. Which leadership qualities do you need to strengthen?

3. Which management skills do you need to improve?

4. How well do you balance vision with execution?

5. What one step can you take this week to grow in both capacities?

ACTION STEPS

1. Identify one leadership behavior you will improve this month.

2. Identify one management skill you will strengthen this month.

3. Seek feedback from your team on your balance of leadership and management.

4. Study one leadership book and one management book this quarter.

5. Apply one new strategy this week that improves both vision and execution.

Closing Thought

Leadership sets the destination. Management builds the road.
Together — they reach the promise.

CHAPTER 39 — Qualifications and Criteria for Selecting Great and Effective Leaders

Introduction

Selecting great and effective leaders is one of the most critical decisions any organization, institution, ministry, or community can make. The success, stability, and sustainability of any group rise or fall on the quality of its leadership. The right leader does more than achieve results — they inspire, empower, model integrity, and cultivate potential in others.

This chapter explores the essential qualifications and criteria for selecting leaders who can drive both immediate performance and long-term legacy, while upholding the highest ethical, moral, and relational standards.

1. VISION AND STRATEGIC THINKING

Qualification:

A leader must possess a clear and compelling vision for the future — the ability to see beyond the present and chart a purposeful course forward.

Criteria:

Look for candidates who demonstrate strategic planning ability, long-term thinking, and the capacity to articulate a vision that mobilizes people toward common goals.

2. INTEGRITY AND ETHICAL STANDARDS

Qualification:

Integrity is the bedrock of leadership. A great leader is honest, trustworthy, and morally consistent.

Criteria:

Evaluate the candidate's reputation for ethical decision-making, transparency, and consistency between words and actions — especially under pressure.

3. EMOTIONAL INTELLIGENCE (EQ)

Qualification:

Emotional intelligence is the ability to understand, manage, and wisely respond to emotions — both personal and relational.

Criteria:

Look for empathy, self-awareness, emotional stability, conflict-management skills, and the ability to build healthy relationships.

4. COMMUNICATION SKILLS

Qualification:

Effective leaders communicate clearly, listen actively, and engage stakeholders meaningfully.

Criteria:

Assess clarity of expression, persuasion ability, listening capacity, and confidence in both verbal and written communication.

5. DECISION-MAKING ABILITY

Qualification:

Leaders must make sound decisions under pressure.

Criteria:

Look for evidence of analytical thinking, discernment, courage in decision-making, and accountability for outcomes.

6. ADAPTABILITY AND RESILIENCE

Qualification:

Effective leaders remain flexible and steady amid change.

Criteria:

Evaluate how the candidate handles uncertainty, setbacks, and transitions while maintaining momentum.

7. ACCOUNTABILITY AND RESPONSIBILITY

Qualification:

Great leaders take ownership of good or bad results.

Criteria:

Assess whether the candidate admits mistakes, learns from failure, and holds themselves and others accountable.

8. INSPIRATIONAL AND MOTIVATIONAL ABILITY

Qualification:

Leaders inspire confidence, purpose, and engagement.

Criteria:

Look for examples of team motivation, culture building, and ability to bring out the best in others.

9. COMMITMENT TO CONTINUOUS LEARNING

Qualification:

The best leaders are lifelong learners.

Criteria:

Evaluate evidence of ongoing personal development, openness to feedback, and intellectual curiosity.

10. RESULTS-ORIENTED FOCUS

Qualification:

Leadership must ultimately produce measurable outcomes.

Criteria:

Assess track record of goal achievement, growth delivery, and performance improvement.

11. TEAM BUILDING AND COLLABORATION

Qualification:

Effective leaders build strong, inclusive, high-performing teams.

Criteria:

Look for experience in mentoring, developing people, and fostering collaboration.

12. CULTURAL FIT

Qualification:

A leader must embody the values and culture of the organization.

Criteria:

Assess alignment of values, beliefs, and behavioral standards with organizational identity.

BIBLICAL PERSPECTIVE ON LEADERSHIP QUALIFICATIONS

Scripture provides timeless guidance on leadership selection:

Character & Integrity "Choose able men who fear God, men of truth." — *Exodus 18:21*

Wisdom & Discernment "Choose wise and understanding men." — *Deuteronomy 1:13*

Servant Leadership "Whoever desires to be great must be a servant." — *Matthew 20:26*

Courage & Conviction "He must hold firmly to sound doctrine." — *Titus 1:9*

Biblical leadership emphasizes character before competence — because skill without integrity becomes dangerous.

13. WHAT PEOPLE LOOK FOR IN LEADERS TODAY

Modern leadership selection prioritizes:

- Integrity

- Vision

- Communication

- Empathy

- Decisiveness

- Accountability

- Innovation

- Courage

- Humility

- Results

Great leaders blend **heart, head, and hands**.

CONTEMPORARY EXAMPLES OF LEADERSHIP QUALITIES

- **Integrity:** Angela Merkel

- **Vision:** Elon Musk

- **Communication:** Barack Obama

- **Emotional Intelligence:** Jacinda Ardern

- **Decision-Making:** Sundar Pichai

- **Accountability:** Satya Nadella

- **Adaptability:** Mary Barra

- **Inspiration:** Malala Yousafzai

- **Humility:** Pope Francis

CONCLUSION

Selecting the right leader requires balancing competence, character, vision, and values. Organizations that prioritize these qualifications build stable futures, strong cultures, and enduring legacies. Whether in business, ministry, government, or community, the right leader makes the difference between progress and decline, unity and division, success and failure. These examples show how leadership qualities manifest in real-world influence. With these criteria in place, we now move to explore the rewards and recognition associated with leadership.

KEY TAKEAWAYS

- Leadership selection determines organizational destiny.

- Character and integrity outweigh charisma alone.

- Vision without execution fails; execution without vision stagnates.

- Emotional intelligence builds trust and loyalty.

- Great leaders grow people while delivering results.

- Biblical principles affirm timeless leadership standards.

REFLECTION QUESTIONS

1. Which leadership qualification do you personally value most — and why?

2. Which of these qualities do you need to develop further?

3. How do you currently evaluate leadership candidates?

4. Are character and competence equally weighed in your selection process?

5. What leadership legacy are you building?

ACTION STEPS

1. Create a leadership selection checklist using these 12 criteria.

2. Assess your current leadership strengths and gaps.

3. Seek mentorship to grow in weak areas.

4. Apply biblical character principles in leadership evaluation.

5. Develop emerging leaders intentionally in your organization.

Closing Thought

Selecting leaders is not about credentials alone, it is about character, capacity, and calling.

PART VI — LEADERSHIP REWARDS & LEGACY

A leader leaves an enduring mark.

CHAPTER 40 — Leadership Rewards and Recognition

Introduction

Leadership is a journey filled with challenges, responsibility, learning, and growth. While the demands of leadership are significant, so too are the rewards. Recognizing and appreciating the contributions of leaders is crucial — not only for the individual leader, but also for the organization and the culture it seeks to build.

Rewards and recognition reinforce excellence, strengthen commitment, and inspire others to rise in leadership. This chapter explores the importance of leadership rewards and recognition, the types of rewards organizations can offer, best practices for effective recognition programs, and how great leaders use recognition to make people feel valued and significant.

1. THE IMPORTANCE OF LEADERSHIP REWARDS AND RECOGNITION

1.1 Motivation and Morale

Recognition boosts morale and motivates leaders to continue striving for excellence. When leaders feel valued, they become more engaged, committed, and enthusiastic in their roles.

1.2 Retention of Top Talent

High-performing leaders who feel appreciated are less likely to seek opportunities elsewhere. Recognition strengthens loyalty and reduces leadership turnover.

1.3 Promotion of Positive Behavior

Rewards reinforce desired leadership behaviors and set visible standards for others to follow, creating a culture where excellence is modeled and emulated.

1.4 Encouragement of Continuous Improvement

Recognition inspires leaders to keep growing, learning, and sharpening their skills, producing ongoing personal and organizational development.

1.5 Fostering a Culture of Appreciation

A recognition-rich culture builds trust, respect, and positive workplace relationships — benefiting leaders, teams, and the entire organization.

2. TYPES OF LEADERSHIP REWARDS

2.1 Financial Rewards

- Performance bonuses
- Salary increases
- Profit-sharing incentives

2.2 Non-Financial Rewards

- Public recognition
- Awards and plaques
- Professional development opportunities

2.3 Personalized Rewards

- Extra vacation or sabbaticals

- Customized gifts

- Executive privileges or flexible schedules

2.4 Career Advancement

- Promotions

- Assignment to major projects

- Expanded leadership responsibility

3. BEST PRACTICES FOR LEADERSHIP RECOGNITION PROGRAMS

1. Align recognition with organizational goals

2. Apply recognition fairly and consistently

3. Make recognition timely

4. Involve peers and team members

5. Tailor recognition to individual preferences

6. Clearly communicate the impact of contributions

7. Celebrate milestones

8. Encourage organization-wide recognition culture

9. Regularly evaluate recognition effectiveness

10. Link recognition to leadership development

4. CHALLENGES IN LEADERSHIP RECOGNITION

- Avoiding recognition fatigue

- Balancing public and private recognition

- Ensuring inclusivity

- Preventing favoritism perceptions

Transparency and intentionality keep recognition meaningful.

5. HOW GREAT LEADERS MAKE PEOPLE FEEL IMPORTANT

Effective leadership is relational. Leaders inspire followership by making people feel valued.

Practical Ways to Show Appreciation:

- Pay attention to people

- Listen actively

- Use positive language

- Write personal notes

- Keep commitments

- Give credit publicly

- Recognize in preferred ways

People will forget what you said, but they will never forget how you made them feel.

6. THE POWER OF RECOGNITION

Recognition is a catalyst for motivation, engagement, and performance.

Mary Kay Ash said:

"People want recognition and praise even more than money."

When leaders recognize contributions, they reinforce excellence and unlock hidden potential.

7. CREATING A CULTURE OF APPRECIATION

Cultures of appreciation are built through:

- Simple courtesy
- Active listening
- Positive language
- Written praise
- Public credit

These practices strengthen belonging and ownership.

8. THE GOLDEN RULE AND THE PLATINUM RULE OF LEADERSHIP

Golden Rule: Treat others as you wish to be treated.
Platinum Rule: Treat others as they wish to be treated.

Great leaders understand individual recognition preferences and honor them accordingly.

9. THE IMPACT OF RECOGNITION ON LEADERSHIP SUCCESS

Recognition drives:

- Higher engagement
- Stronger commitment
- Improved performance
- Healthier team dynamics
- Sustainable organizational growth

As Dwight Frindt stated:

"Acknowledgment and celebration fuel passion, validate effort, and give teams a real sense of progress."

CONCLUSION

Leadership rewards and recognition are not optional extras
— they are strategic leadership tools. By acknowledging
dedication, achievement, and effort, organizations
motivate, retain, and inspire their leaders. More
importantly, recognition builds cultures where excellence
becomes normal and legacy is sustained.

True leadership is not only about guiding people toward goals
— it is about making them feel valued along the journey.
Understanding the rewards of leadership now leads us to
explore the concept of leadership legacy.

KEY **TAKEAWAYS**

- Recognition fuels motivation and loyalty.

- Appreciated leaders stay committed.

- Rewarded behavior is repeated behavior.

- Personal recognition creates lasting impact.

- Cultures of appreciation produce high performance.

- Legacy-minded leaders celebrate others' success.

REFLECTION QUESTIONS

1. How do you recognize leadership contributions?

2. What type of recognition motivates you personally?

3. Are your recognition practices fair and consistent?

4. How can you make your team feel more valued?

5. What culture of appreciation are you building?

ACTION STEPS

1. Design a simple leadership recognition plan for your organization.

2. Identify three leaders to intentionally appreciate this month.

3. Ask team members how they prefer to be recognized.

4. Write one handwritten appreciation note this week.

5. Celebrate one milestone publicly.

Closing Thought

Leadership is not just about achieving results—it is about making people feel valued along the journey and inspiring them to rise.

CHAPTER 41 — Leadership Legacy

Introduction

A leader's legacy is not defined solely by what they accomplish during their tenure, but by the lasting impact they leave behind. Leadership legacy encompasses the influence, contributions, and values that endure long after a leader has stepped aside. It is about building something that outlives personal presence — a culture, an organization, a movement, or a generation of empowered leaders.

True leaders think beyond immediate success. They ask: **"What will remain because I led-"**

This chapter explores the meaning of leadership legacy, the elements that shape it, practical strategies for building it, challenges leaders face along the way, and real-world examples of enduring leadership impact.

1. THE CONCEPT OF LEADERSHIP LEGACY

1.1 Defining Leadership Legacy

Leadership legacy is the enduring imprint a leader leaves on people, organizations, and society. It reflects the values lived, decisions made, culture built, and lives transformed — all of which continue influencing the future.

1.2 Why Leadership Legacy Matters

Legacy matters because leadership is stewardship. Every leader temporarily holds responsibility for people and resources that will outlast them. A strong legacy inspires future generations, guides organizational direction, and preserves purpose beyond leadership transition.

1.3 Legacy as the True Measure of Leadership Success

Short-term achievements fade, but legacy endures — the true test of leadership success is what continues to thrive after the leader is gone.

Example:
Nelson Mandela's legacy of reconciliation, justice, and unity continues shaping global leadership long after his lifetime.

2. ELEMENTS OF A LEADERSHIP LEGACY

2.1 Values and Principles

A leader's core values form the foundation of their legacy. Integrity, fairness, empathy, courage, and service become guiding standards for future generations.

Example: Mahatma Gandhi's unwavering commitment to nonviolence created a timeless leadership legacy.

2.2 Organizational Culture

Leaders leave legacy through culture — the behaviors, attitudes, and norms that define "how things are done here."

Example: Herb Kelleher built Southwest Airlines on a people-first culture that still defines the company today.

2.3 Mentorship and Developing Future Leaders

The greatest leadership legacy is people. Leaders who develop others multiply their influence far beyond their own lifespan.

Example: Jack Welch's leadership development culture at GE produced generations of global CEOs.

2.4 Achievements and Innovations

Transformational initiatives and innovations often become lasting symbols of a leader's tenure.

Example: Steve Jobs' innovations at Apple permanently reshaped global technology and design culture.

2.5 Social Impact and Community Contribution

Leaders who improve society leave legacies that transcend business or organizational walls.

Example: Oprah Winfrey's philanthropy and empowerment initiatives continue transforming lives worldwide.

2.6 Ethical Decision-Making

Leaders who uphold strong ethical standards establish cultures of trust that endure.

Example: Warren Buffett's commitment to ethical investing set a benchmark for business integrity.

3. HOW TO BUILD A LASTING LEADERSHIP LEGACY

3.1 Lead with Vision and Purpose

A meaningful legacy begins with clarity of vision. Leaders who know why they lead create directions that others continue following.

3.2 Build a Strong Culture

Culture outlives strategy. Leaders who intentionally shape culture create enduring organizational identity.

3.3 Develop and Empower Others

Leadership legacy is measured in successors — empowering others ensures continuity.

3.4 Prioritize Integrity

Legacy built without integrity collapses. Trust is the currency of enduring leadership influence.

3.5 Drive Positive Change and Innovation

Progressive leaders leave organizations stronger, smarter, and better prepared for the future.

3.6 Remain Authentic and Consistent

Consistence between values, words, and actions establishes credibility that withstands time.

3. 7 Give Back to Society

Leaders who serve beyond self-interest plant seeds of impact far into the future.

4. CHALLENGES IN LEAVING LEADERSHIP LEGACY

- Balancing short-term results with long-term impact
- Preparing and trusting successors
- Facing criticism and resistance
- Staying relevant across changing times
- Avoiding ego-driven leadership

Legacy-focused leaders lead for impact, not applause.

5. REAL-WORLD EXAMPLES OF LEADERSHIP LEGACY

- **Nelson Mandela** — Reconciliation and justice
- **Bill Gates** — Innovation and philanthropy
- **Walt Disney** — Creativity and imagination
- **Mother Teresa** — Compassion and service
- **Rosa Parks** — Courage and equality

Each left a legacy that outlived their presence.

CONCLUSION

Leadership legacy is not built at the end of leadership — it is built every day. It is seen in the developed people, the culture shaped, the integrity upheld, and the vision passed forward.

A leader's greatness is not measured by how many follow them, but by how many rises because of them.

As John C. Maxwell states:

"A leader's lasting value is measured by succession."

Those who lead with purpose, integrity, and service leave footprints that guide generations yet unborn. Building a legacy now prepares us to examine the importance of leadership succession.

6. KEY TAKEAWAYS

- Leadership legacy is measured by lasting impact.

- Values form the foundation of legacy.

- People development is the greatest legacy investment.

- Culture is a leader's silent signature.

- Integrity preserves leadership influence.

- True leaders build successors, not dependence.

7. REFLECTION QUESTIONS

1. What kind of legacy do I want to leave?

2. What values will define my leadership story?

3. Who am I intentionally developing as future leaders?

4. What culture am I building through my daily actions?

5. If I left today, what would remain because I led?

8. ACTION STEPS

1. Write a personal leadership legacy statement.

2. Identify three people you will mentor this year.

3. Define the core values you want your team to live by.

4. Start one initiative that will outlast your tenure.

5. Evaluate decisions by asking: "Does this build legacy-"

Closing Thought

Your leadership is temporary, but your legacy is lasting. Build what will outlive you.

CHAPTER 42 — Leadership Succession

Introduction

Leadership succession is one of the most critical elements of organizational stability, longevity, and sustained excellence. Every leadership role is temporary; therefore, every leader must think beyond personal tenure and prepare others to carry the mission forward. Leadership succession is the intentional process of identifying, developing, and positioning future leaders to step into key roles when transition becomes necessary.

Organizations that fail to plan for succession risk disruption, loss of institutional knowledge, and instability. Conversely, organizations that prioritize succession planning create continuity, confidence, and a culture of leadership development at every level.

This chapter explores the importance of leadership succession, the succession planning process, best practices, common challenges, real-world examples, and how leaders can ensure their influence continues beyond their time in office.

1. THE IMPORTANCE OF LEADERSHIP SUCCESSION

1.1 Ensuring Continuity and Stability

Succession planning ensures smooth leadership transitions. When successors are prepared in advance, organizations avoid disruption, confusion, and loss of momentum during leadership change.

1.2 Preserving Institutional Knowledge

Effective succession transfers wisdom, experience, organizational memory, and cultural understanding from current leaders to emerging ones, preventing knowledge loss.

1.3 Retaining and Motivating Talent

Clear succession pathways show employees that growth and advancement are possible. This increases engagement, reduces turnover, and strengthens morale.

1.4 Fostering a Culture of Development

Organizations that emphasize succession naturally build cultures of continuous learning, mentorship, and leadership excellence.

1.5 Strengthening Organizational Agility

Prepared successors allow organizations to respond confidently to crisis, opportunity, or unexpected change.

2. THE SUCCESSION PLANNING PROCESS

2.1 Identify Key Leadership Roles

Determine which roles are critical to mission, strategy, and operational stability.

2.2 Assess Leadership Requirements

Define the skills, competencies, character traits, and future-oriented capabilities required for each leadership role.

2.3 Identify Potential Successors

Recognize high-potential individuals based on performance, leadership traits, cultural alignment, and growth capacity.

2.4 Create Development Pathways

Provide mentoring, coaching, training, job rotation, and leadership assignments to prepare successors.

2.5 Monitor Progress

Evaluate development regularly through feedback, assessments, and performance reviews.

2.6 Formalize the Succession Plan

Document succession strategies, transition procedures, and contingency plans.

3. BEST PRACTICES FOR LEADERSHIP SUCCESSION

- Begin succession planning early
- Involve current leaders in mentoring successors
- Combine internal development with external talent when necessary
- Focus on competency and character, not tenure alone
- Provide stretch assignments
- Encourage cross-functional exposure
- Communicate succession plans transparently
- Embed succession into organizational culture
- Review and refine plans regularly

4. CHALLENGES IN LEADERSHIP SUCCESSION

- Resistance to releasing authority

- Bias in successor selection

- Overemphasis on technical skills

- Inadequate development preparation

- Ignoring cultural alignment

Effective succession requires humility, objectivity, and intentional preparation.

5. IMPACT OF A WELL-EXECUTED SUCCESSION PLAN

5.1 Smooth Transitions

Leadership change occurs with confidence and stability.

5.2 Increased Employee Engagement

People see opportunity for advancement and invest in growth.

5.3 Stronger Culture

Successors preserve and strengthen core values.

5.4 Competitive Advantage

Organizations respond faster to change and opportunity.

5.5 Long-Term Sustainability

Leadership pipelines secure enduring success.

6. REAL-WORLD EXAMPLES OF SUCCESSION

Apple — Steve Jobs to Tim Cook A prepared successor preserved innovation and continuity.

General Electric — Leadership Pipeline. A world-renowned leadership factory producing global CEOs.

McDonald's — Internal Leadership Growth

Promotion from within maintained brand consistency and
adaptability.

CONCLUSION

Leadership succession is not an event — it is a responsibility.
Great leaders do not cling to power; they prepare others
to carry it forward. They understand that true leadership
influence is measured not by how long they remain in
position, but by how well the organization thrives after
they are gone.

As the saying goes:

**"Leadership is not about making yourself
indispensable; it is about making yourself
replaceable."**

Leaders who embrace succession think secure continuity,
stability, and sustain excellence. Their greatest
achievement is not holding leadership — but multiplying
leaders. With succession in mind, we now explore the
most important words that define leadership.

7. KEY TAKEAWAYS

- Every leader is temporary — succession is essential.

- Succession preserves knowledge and culture.

- Developing successors multiplies leadership impact.

- Preparation prevents disruption.

- Legacy-focused leaders build replacement, not
  dependence.

8. REFLECTION QUESTIONS

1. If I left today, who is ready to replace me?

2. Am I developing future leaders or protecting my position?

3. What knowledge must I intentionally transfer?

4. Does my organization have a clear succession plan?

5. What leadership talent am I currently mentoring?

9. ACTION STEPS

1. Identify one potential successor to mentor this year.

2. Document key knowledge only you currently hold.

3. Assign stretch leadership opportunities to emerging leaders.

4. Create a written succession plan for your team.

5. Evaluate progress quarterly.

Closing Thought:

Great leaders are not remembered for how long they led, but for who they raised. Leadership finds its highest expression not in holding power, but in passing it on.

CHAPTER 43 — The Most Important Words of a Leader

Introduction

Leadership is not demonstrated only by decisions and actions — it is revealed through words. Every day, leaders speak vision into existence, shape culture through conversation, and influence morale through tone. Words can heal or harm, inspire or discourage, unite or divide.

Great leaders understand that communication is not merely about speaking — it is about connecting. The words a leader chooses reflect character, mindset, and values. More importantly, those words determine how people feel, think, and act.

This chapter explores the most important words every leader must master, why they matter, and how intentional language transforms ordinary leadership into extraordinary influence.

The Power of Words in Leadership

Words build atmosphere. They frame reality. They create belief. A leader's words can:

- Spark motivation
- Strengthen trust
- Encourage innovation
- Resolve conflict
- Reinforce purpose
- Or they can:

- Create fear

- Damage morale

- Breed mistrust

- Suppress creativity

Effective leadership communication is never accidental — it is intentional. Leaders who choose their words wisely shape cultures where people feel valued, engaged, and empowered.

The Most Important Words of a Leader

"We" — The Word of Unity

Significance:
"We" is the language of inclusion. It removes ego and reinforces shared purpose.

Impact:
Builds teamwork, collective ownership, and a strong sense of belonging.

"Thank You" — The Word of Appreciation

Significance:
Gratitude acknowledges effort and honors contribution.

Impact:
Boosts morale, strengthens loyalty, and reinforces a positive culture.

"Please" — The Word of Respect

Significance:
Politeness communicates dignity and value.

Impact:

Creates cooperation, reduces resistance, and fosters mutual respect.

"How Can I Help-" — The Word of Servant Leadership

Significance:

Signals support and approachability.

Impact:

Builds trust, encourages openness, and reinforces servant leadership.

"I Believe in You" — The Word of Empowerment

Significance:

Affirms confidence in others.

Impact:

Builds self-belief, courage, and high performance.

"What Do You Think-" — The Word of Inclusion

Significance:

Invites participation and ownership.

Impact:

Encourages creativity, innovation, and collaborative decision-making.

"I'm Sorry" — The Word of Humility

Significance:

Acknowledges mistakes and models accountability.

Impact:

Builds credibility, restores trust, and encourages a learning culture.

"Let's" — The Word of Shared Action

Significance:

Positions the leader as part of the team.

Impact:

Promotes unity, shared responsibility, and momentum.

"Yes" — The Word of Possibility

Significance:

Opens doors to opportunity.

Impact:

Encourages innovation, optimism, and boldness.

"No" — The Word of Focus

Significance:

Protects priorities and boundaries.

Impact:

Prevents distraction, burnout, and misaligned effort.

The Classic Leadership Word Scale

This timeless leadership scale captures the spirit of effective communication:

Six most important words: "I admit I made a mistake."

Five most important words: "You did a good job."

Four most important words: "What do you think-"

Three most important words: "I take responsibility."

Two most important words: "Thank you."

One most important word:

"We."

Least important word:" I."

The quality of your leadership is reflected in the words you choose most often.

Why These Words Matter

- They reduce ego

- They increase trust

- They promote accountability

- They strengthen relationships

- They inspire ownership

- They reinforce servant leadership

- They create emotionally intelligent cultures

Language shapes leadership reality.

A true leader understands: **If the team wins, the leader wins.**
If the team fails, the leader takes responsibility.

The Leadership Language Principle

Poor Leader: "I achieved this." Great Leader: "We achieved this."

Poor Leader: "My vision." Great Leader: "Our vision."

Poor Leader: "Do what I say." Great Leader: "Let's do this together."

Core Leadership Truth

Leadership is not about being the star. It is about making the team shine.

When a leader replaces **"I"** with **"We, "**they move from self-promotion to legacy-building.

CONCLUSION

Leadership is revealed in language before it is proven in action. The most effective leaders do not merely give instructions — they speak belief, purpose, courage, and unity into the hearts of people.

When leaders master their words, they master influence. When they speak with humility, gratitude, and vision, they transform workplaces, communities, and destinies.

Choose your words wisely — because your words become your leadership legacy. These defining words now lead us to reflect on leadership through self-assessment.

KEY TAKEAWAYS

- Words are powerful leadership tools that shape culture, morale, and performance

- Inclusive language ("we") builds unity, ownership, and belonging

- Gratitude, respect, and encouragement strengthen trust and motivation

- Humility and accountability increase credibility and influence

- Asking for input empowers teams and fosters innovation

- Boundaries protect focus and preserve leadership effectiveness

- Great leaders use words to build people, not create fear

REFLECTION QUESTIONS

1. What words do I use most often as a leader — "I" or "we"?

2. Do my words build people or pressure them?

3. How often do I intentionally express gratitude to others?

4. When last did I say,"I was wrong" or "I'm sorry"?

5. Do my words make people feel safe, valued, and heard?

6. Do I regularly ask for input from others before making decisions?

7. What one word or phrase could I start using more to strengthen my leadership?

ACTION STEPS

1. Practice "We" Language Daily
Consciously replace "I" and "my" with "we" and "our" in your communication.

2. Express Daily Gratitude
Thank at least one person each day for a specific contribution.

3. Invite Participation
Ask,"What do you think?" before making key decisions.

4. Offer Support
   Ask someone, "How can I help?" and follow through.

5. Affirm Potential
   Encourage at least one person daily with intentional words.

6. Model Humility
   Admit mistakes openly and apologize when necessary.

7. Audit Your Words Weekly
   Reflect: Did my words build confidence or diminish it?

CLOSING LEADERSHIP INSIGHT

The strongest leaders speak less about themselves and more about their teams.

The word "We" builds organizations.
The word "I" builds ego.

Legacy leaders choose "We."

Champion Remain.

CHAPTER 44 — Leadership Assessment

Introduction

Leadership assessment is a critical process that enables leaders to understand their strengths, weaknesses, and areas for growth. Through structured tools and reflective methods, leaders gain valuable insight into their leadership style, effectiveness, and impact on their teams and organizations.

Effective leaders do not guess their growth areas — they measure them.

Leadership assessment transforms intention into improvement and potential into performance. This chapter explores the importance of leadership assessment, the major types of assessment tools available, and how to interpret and apply results to enhance leadership effectiveness.

1. Importance of Leadership Assessment

Leadership assessment is essential for several reasons:

Self-Awareness

Assessment helps leaders gain deeper understanding of their personal traits, behavioral tendencies, emotional patterns, and leadership style — leading to increased self-awareness.

Performance Improvement

By identifying development areas, leaders can focus on specific skills and behaviors that improve their overall effectiveness.

Team Dynamics

Understanding how leadership style affects team performance allows leaders to adjust their approach to better meet team needs.

Organizational Success

Effective leadership directly influences organizational success. Regular assessment ensures leaders remain aligned with organizational goals, values, and culture.

2. Types of Leadership Assessments

Different assessment tools serve different developmental purposes:

Self-Assessment

Reflective questionnaires and rating scales that help leaders evaluate their own behaviors and leadership tendencies.

360-Degree Feedback

Feedback gathered from supervisors, peers, and subordinates, providing a well-rounded view of leadership impact.

Personality Assessments

Tools such as MBTI or Big Five Personality Traits that reveal personality-driven leadership preferences.

Behavioral Assessments

Measurements focused on observable leadership behaviors such as communication, delegation, conflict resolution, and decision-making.

Situational Judgment Tests

Scenario-based evaluations that assess how leaders respond to real-world leadership challenges.

Emotional Intelligence (EI) Assessments

Tools such as EQ-i that measure emotional intelligence — one of the strongest predictors of leadership effectiveness.

3. Interpreting Assessment Results

Assessment results become valuable only when properly interpreted:

Identify Strengths

Recognize areas of excellence and intentionally leverage these strengths in leadership practice.

Spot Development Areas

Acknowledge skills needing improvement and commit to targeted growth.

Creating a Development Plan

Translate insights into a personalized leadership development plan with clear goals, actions, and timelines.

Seeking Feedback

Discuss results with mentors, coaches, or trusted colleagues for external perspective and accountability.

4. Implementing Change Based on Assessment

To apply assessment insights effectively:

Set Clear Goals

Define SMART (Specific, Measurable, Achievable, Relevant, Time-bound) development objectives.

Engage in Continuous Learning

Pursuing training, coaching, reading, and experiential learning aligned with growth areas.

Monitor Progress

Track improvement regularly and adjust strategies when necessary.

Reassessed Periodically

Conduct follow-up assessments to measure progress and recalibrate development plans.

5. The Role of Organizations in Leadership Assessment

Organizations play a vital role in supporting leadership growth:

Provide Resources

Offer access to assessment tools and leadership development programs.

Encourage Participation

Promote regular leadership assessment as part of professional development culture.

Creating a Feedback Culture

Build environments where constructive feedback is welcomed and used for growth.

Align Assessments with Organizational Goals

Ensure assessment frameworks reflect organizational values, competencies, and strategic direction.

6. Conclusion

Leadership assessment is not a one-time event — it is an ongoing process that keeps leaders growing, adapting, and remaining effective in evolving environments.

Leaders who assess regularly improve intentionally. Leaders who improve intentionally build legacy.

Continuous assessment and continuous improvement are hallmarks of truly impactful leadership. Through assessment, we now draw from timeless leadership wisdom that has guided leaders across generations.

LEADERSHIP SELF-ASSESSMENT INSTRUMENT

Instructions

Rate yourself on a scale of 1 to 5:

1 = Strongly Disagree
  2 = Disagree
  3 = Neutral
  4 = Agree
  5 = Strongly Agree

Section 1 — Vision and Strategic Thinking

1. I have a clear vision for my team or organization.

2. I effectively communicate my vision to others.

3. I set long-term goals aligned with my vision.

4. I regularly review and adjust strategy.

5. I inspire others toward a common vision.

Section 2 — Communication Skills

6. I communicate clearly with my team.

7. I listen actively to others' viewpoints.

8. I provide constructive feedback.

9. I handle conflicts with tact and diplomacy.

10. I encourage open communication.

Section 3 — Decision-Making and Problem-Solving

11. I make decisions confidently.

12. I consider stakeholder impact.

13. I involve others when appropriate.

14. I solve complex problems effectively.

15. I balance data and intuition.

Section 4 — Emotional Intelligence

16. I am aware of my emotions.

17. I manage stress effectively.

18. I empathize with others.

19. I build trust-based relationships.

20. I handle interpersonal conflict fairly.

Section 5 — Team Leadership and Development

21. I build collaborative teams.

22. I recognize team strengths.

23. I develop others' potential.

24. I delegate effectively.

25. I celebrate team success.

Section 6 — Ethical Leadership

26. I uphold high ethical standards.

27. I lead by example.

28. I make fair decisions.

29. I hold myself accountable.

30. I address unethical behavior.

Section 7 — Adaptability and Growth

31. I adapt to change quickly.

32. I encourage innovation.

33. I adjusted leadership style as needed.

34. I handle challenges positively.

35. I seek continuous improvement.

Scoring Guide

150–175 — Exceptional Leader
125–149 — Strong Leader
100–124 — Developing Leader
75–99 — Emerging Leader
Below 75 — Leadership Potential Stage

Next Steps

- Reflect on highest and lowest scoring areas
- Set development goals
- Create an action plan

- Seek mentor feedback• Reassess every 6–12 months

KEY TAKEAWAYS

End-of-Chapter Takeaways

- Leadership growth begins with self-awareness

- Assessment reveals blind spots and strengths

- Feedback accelerates leadership maturity

- Development must be intentional

- Great leaders measure before they improve

REFLECTION QUESTIONS

1. What did this assessment reveal about me?

2. Which leadership strength must I leverage more?

3. Which development area needs immediate attention?

4. Who will hold me accountable for growth?

5. When will I reassess my progress?

ACTION STEPS

1. Complete the self-assessment honestly.

2. Identify your top two strengths and top two growth areas.

3. Write a 90-day leadership development plan.

4. Seek feedback from one mentor or coach.

5. Schedule your next reassessment date.

CLOSING LEADERSHIP INSIGHT

Leaders who refuse to assess stagnate. Leaders who assess grow.
Leaders who grow leave legacy.

CHAPTER 45 — Timeless Leadership Quotes: Wisdom to Lead, Live, and Leave a Legacy

Introduction

Every great movement, organization, and transformation begins with a thought. Every enduring legacy is built on guiding principles that shape daily decisions.

Throughout *What Every Leader Must Know*, we have explored the heart, mind, and practice of leadership. This final chapter gathers essential leadership truths into concise and memorable statements — quotes designed to inspire reflection, ignite courage, and reinforce purpose.

Return to these words often. Let them anchor your journey as you grow from potential to performance, from vision to impact, and from obscurity to significance.

45 Timeless Leadership Quotes

1. Leadership is not about position; it is about responsibility.

2. You cannot lead others beyond the level at which you lead yourself.

3. Vision gives direction, but character gives permission to lead.

4. A leader's greatest assignment is to awaken greatness in others.

5. Influence is earned through service, not demanded by title.

6. Where purpose is clear, persistence becomes natural.

7. Great leaders create more leaders, not more followers.

8. Self-discipline is the silent engine of leadership success.

9. If you cannot manage your emotions, you cannot manage your influence.

10. Leadership begins the moment you take ownership of your life.

11. A leader who stops learning stops leading.

12. Courage is not the absence of fear; it is obedience in spite of fear.

13. Vision without action is a dream; action without vision is confusion.

14. Excellence is not an event — it is the daily habit of great leaders.

15. People follow leaders who value them before they need them.

16. The true test of leadership is what remains after you are gone.

17. Integrity is the foundation upon which influence is built.

18. Leadership is lifting others to see what they could not see alone.

19. A leader's words shape culture; a leader's actions define it.

20. Pressure reveals character, not talent.

21. Do not despise small beginnings — every giant started as a seed.

22. Leaders go first — in vision, in sacrifice, and in example.

23. You grow into leadership by growing in humility.

24. Consistency separates good leaders from great ones.

25. Service is the highest expression of leadership.

26. When values are clear, decisions become easier.

27. Your personal vision must be stronger than your present reality.

28. Leadership is stewardship — you are entrusted, not entitled.

29. The measure of leadership is not popularity, but impact.

30. A leader's private life determines their public strength.

31. People may forget your words, but they will never forget how you made them feel.

32. True leaders build bridges, not walls.

33. Your response to failure determines your future influence.

34. Leadership is faith in action.

35. If you want to change an organization, first change the atmosphere.

36. A leader sees potential where others see problems.

37. Your assignment is always bigger than your comfort zone.

38. Leaders multiply vision by empowering others.

39. Time reveals who is truly committed to the vision.

40. Great leaders listen more than they speak.

41. The price of leadership is paid before the rewards appear.

42. You lead best where passion and purpose meet.

43. Legacy is leadership that outlives you.

44. A leader's greatest victory is seeing others surpass them.

45. You were born to lead — but leadership is chosen daily.

The Most Important Word of a Leader

"WE."

The greatest leaders speak in *We*, not *I*.
Leadership is never about personal glory.
It is about the team, the mission, and the shared journey.

The wasted words of leadership are *"I"* and *"Me."*
A self-centered leader limits influence. A team-centered leader multiplies impact.

True leadership is inclusive. True leadership is collective.
True leadership is **WE**.

CLOSING REFLECTIONS

Leadership is a journey, not a destination. It is practiced in daily decisions, proven in adversity, refined through service, and fulfilled in legacy.

May these words remind you that leadership is not reserved for the few — it is the calling of all who dare to live with purpose, serve with humility, and rise with courage. With this wisdom in mind, we now come to the final charge — an invitation to live out leadership fully.

Champion Remain.

KEY TAKEAWAYS

End-of-Chapter Takeaways

- Leadership principles must be revisited regularly to stay aligned.

- Words shape culture, choose them wisely.

- Great leadership is inclusive, never self-centered.

- Legacy is built daily through consistent action.

- The greatest leaders multiply leaders, not followers.

REFLECTION QUESTIONS

1. Which quote speaks most strongly to your current season of leadership?

2. What personal habit must you develop to live these truths?

3. Where have you used "I" when you should have used "We"?

4. What legacy are you intentionally building starting today?

5. How will those you lead remember your influence?

ACTION STEPS

1. Select one quote to meditate on each week.

2. Replace "I" with "We" in leadership conversations.

3. Write your personal leadership legacy statement.

- Identify one person you will intentionally mentor this month.

- Review this chapter quarterly to recalibrate your leadership journey.

CLOSING THOUGHT

The world does not need more followers. It needs courageous leaders who serve, inspire, and transform.

Go forth — Lead with purpose.

Live with excellence.

Leave a legacy.

CHAPTER 46 — The Final Charge: Becoming the Leader You Were Born to Be

"The greatest leader is not the one who does the
greatest things, but the one who inspires others
to do the greatest things."
— Ronald Reagan

Introduction

Every book has a final page. But leadership has no final
chapter.

What you have read in *What Every Leader Must Know* is not
merely information — it is an invitation. An invitation to
rise above mediocrity, embrace responsibility, live with
purpose, and lead with conviction.

Leadership is not a destination reached. It is a journey chosen
— daily.

This concluding chapter gathers the heart of this book: self-
leadership, vision, character, influence, service,
succession, and legacy — the pillars upon which great
leaders stand.

Leadership Story

The Leader Who Multiplied Leaders

A leader once built a successful organization admired for its
growth, performance, and influence. Many praised his
vision, discipline, and results.

But his greatest test came not during his leadership — but at
his departure.

When he stepped down, something remarkable happened.

The organization did not decline.

It grew stronger.

Why?

Because he had invested years developing people, mentoring future leaders, and building systems that did not depend on him alone.

He understood a powerful truth:

Leadership is not proven by how long you lead — but by what remains after you leave.

His legacy was not position.

His legacy was people.

Leadership Insight

The highest level of leadership is not success — it is succession. True leadership multiplies itself through others.

Application

Begin building your legacy today:

- Mentor intentionally

- Delegate meaningfully

- Develop future leaders

- Document knowledge and systems

Do not build followers — build leaders who will carry the vision forward.

1. Leadership Begins with You

Before you lead others, you must lead yourself. Your habits, mindset, discipline, integrity, and consistency form the foundation of your influence. The person you are becoming is the leader others will follow.

Commit daily to growth. Guard your character. Refine your skills.
Strengthen your vision.

Leadership always starts from the inside out.

2. Leadership Is About People

Leadership is not about power. Not about title. Not about recognition.

Leadership is about people.

- Seeing potential in others
- Speaking life into their purpose
- Creating environments where they flourish
- Empowering them to exceed you

The greatest leaders do not build followers.
They build leaders.

3. Leadership Requires Courage

Every meaningful step in leadership demands courage:

- Courage to speak truth
- Courage to take responsibility
- Courage to fail forward
- Courage to challenge the status quo

- Courage to stand alone when necessary

Fear is natural.

But obedience to purpose is greater.

4. Leadership Demands Service

True leadership kneels before it stands tall.

You lead best when you serve first.

You influence most when you care genuinely.

You rise highest when you lift others.

Service is not weakness.

Service is leadership's highest expression.

5. Leadership Creates Legacy

Your leadership will be remembered — not merely by achievements, but by:

- The culture you built

- The people you developed

- The values you lived

- The leaders you raised

- The lives you impacted

Legacy is leadership that outlives you.

Build it intentionally.

6. Leadership Must Be Passed On

Great leaders do not cling to power.

They prepare successors.

They share knowledge.

They multiply capacity.

They make themselves replaceable.

Succession is the final proof of leadership maturity.

7. Your Leadership Assignment Is Unique

No one carries your exact experiences, gifts, passions, and
calling.
You were placed in this generation for a reason.

Your environment is your assignment. Your influence is your
responsibility. Your vision is your mandate.

Do not shrink back. Step forward.

8. Final Charge

Leadership is not reserved for the extraordinary. It is the daily
choice of the willing. Choose growth over comfort.
Choose service over ego. Choose integrity over
convenience. Choose vision over fear. Choose legacy over
applause. And above all — choose to lead.

Final Blessing

May your vision stay clear. May your courage remain strong.
May your character stay pure. May your influence grow
wide. May your service lift many. May your legacy endure
long after you are gone.

Closing Words

This is not the end of your leadership journey. It is the
beginning of your next level. Go forward. Lead boldly.
Serve humbly. Live purposefully. Leave a legacy.

Champion Remain.

Back Matter

CALL TO ACTION — YOUR LEADERSHIP ASSIGNMENT STARTS NOW

Knowledge without action changes nothing. This book has equipped you — now it is time to apply what you have learned.

Starting today:

- Lead yourself before leading others
- Replace "I" with "We"
- Serve before seeking recognition
- Build people, not platforms
- Think legacy, not applause

Your leadership assignment begins now. Take responsibility. Take initiative. Take the lead.

Champion Remain

CONTINUE YOUR LEADERSHIP JOURNEY

Leadership growth never ends.

- Read at least one leadership book per month

- Seek mentorship and accountability

- Practice reflection and self-assessment

- Develop emerging leaders around you

- Revisit this book quarterly as your leadership compass

Great leaders remain students for life.

READER APPRECIATION & REVIEW REQUEST

Thank you for investing your time in this book.
> If this work has inspired, equipped, or encouraged you, please share your experience by leaving a review or recommending it to others.

Your feedback helps extend this message to leaders across the world.

UPCOMING BOOKS BY AARON PREMPEH

- Becoming Like Christ — Building Unshakable Christian Character

- Principles of Godly Prosperity — Keys to Abundant Living

- Gateway to Ghana — The Complete Travel Guide to West Africa's Hidden Gem

- Raising Generational Blessings

- The Courage to Move Forward

- Out of the Shadows — A Journey of Hope and Redemption

- Parent Leadership — Building Strong Families Through Influence

- Leadership for Youth and Emerging Leaders

- Divine Prosperity Unveiled

(Books, devotionals, workbooks, and coaching programs available through Purpose Givers Publications.)

APPENDIX — LEADERSHIP TOOLS & QUICK REFERENCE

A. Personal Leadership Development Plan

Define your vision, growth goals, learning schedule, and accountability structure.

B. Leadership Self-Assessment Checklist

Evaluate your leadership effectiveness in the following areas:

- Vision

- Communication

- Emotional intelligence

- Decision-making

- Integrity

- Service

C. Vision Execution Framework

Vision → Strategy → Action → Consistency → Results → Legacy

C. Legacy Planning Worksheet

- What values will I be remembered for?

- Who am I developing to succeed me?

- What culture am I building?

- What impact will remain after?

- What impact will remain after?

- I am gone?

  Note: Printable worksheets for these tools are available in the
  Workbook Edition of this book.

THE ONE-PAGE LEADER'S GUIDE

A Quick Daily Leadership Compass

1. **Vision**
   - Do I know where I am going?
   - Have I clearly communicated the direction?

2. **Character**
   - Am I leading with integrity and consistency?
   - Do my actions match my values?

3. **People**
   - Am I developing others or just directing them?
   - Have I encouraged someone today?

4. **Execution**
   - Are plans turning into action?
   - Am I holding myself and others accountable?

5. **Service**
   - Am I serving before seeking recognition?

6. **Growth**
   - What did I learn today that improved my leadership?

Daily Leadership Reminder:

Lead yourself first.

Serve people genuinely.

Execute vision faithfully.

Build legacy intentionally.

— Aaron Prempeh

REFERENCES

1. Mills, D. Q. (2005). *Leadership: How to Lead, How to Live.*

2. Engstrom, T. W. (1976). *The Making of a Christian Leader.* Zondervan.

3. Bass, B. (1990). *From Transactional to Transformational Leadership.*

4. Kouzes, J. & Posner, B. (1987). *The Leadership Challenge.*

5. Northouse, G. (2007). *Leadership Theory and Practice.*

6. Maxwell, J. C. (2007). *The 21 Irrefutable Laws of Leadership.*

7. Covey, S. R. *The 7 Habits of Highly Effective People.*

8. Drucker, P. *The Practice of Management.*

9. Munroe, M. *Principles of Eagles.*

10. Holy Bible (KJV). Proverbs 11:14.

WHERE TO GET THIS BOOK

What Every Leader Must Know: The Essentials of Empowering Leadership is available worldwide in Paperback, Hardcover, eBook, and Special Editions through major global platforms:

Confirmed Current Online Listings

- Walmart (Paperback – Online Retail)
- Amazon (Global including Amazon Singapore)
- Everand (eBook Platform)

Major Global Book Retailers

- Amazon Worldwide
- Barnes & Noble
- Apple Books
- Google Play Books
- Kobo / Rakuten Kobo
- Books-A-Million
- Target Books (Online)

Discovery & Review Platforms

- Goodreads
- BookBub
- Library Thing

Library & Institutional Networks

- Ingram Spark Partner Bookstores

- Overdrive / Libby

- Hoopla Digital

Direct Author Stores

- aaronprempeh.com

- aaronprempehbooks.com

- purposegivers.co

Bulk, corporate, and ministry orders are available through Purpose Givers Publications.

ABOUT THE AUTHOR

Aaron Duah Agyeman Prempeh, professionally known as

Aaron Prempeh, is a Ghanaian -American author, leadership coach, speaker, and transformational mentor based in the United States. A certified John Maxwell Coach, Teacher, and Speaker, he equips individuals and organizations to grow in leadership, purpose, and lasting impact across business, community, and faith environments.

He is Founder and President of Purpose Givers LLC (USA), Purpose Givers Ltd (UK & Ghana), Focusline Company Limited (Ghana), and Executive Director of Generational Thinkers International, an NGO committed to raising a new generation of visionary leaders.

Aaron integrates timeless biblical principles with practical leadership strategies to inspire ethical, purpose-driven,

and servant-hearted leadership. His mission is to raise
generational leaders who lead with integrity, serve with
excellence, and build legacies that transform nations.

He brings over three decades of experience across aviation,
banking, sales, customer service, project management,
and Agile leadership environments, with professional
roles at KLM Royal Dutch Airlines, JP Morgan Chase,
Huntington National Bank, Sears Home Improvement,
CarMax (President's Club Member), and Systems
Unlimited Inc.

He holds an Executive MBA from Kwame Nkrumah
University of Science and Technology (Ghana), and
certifications in John Maxwell Coaching, SAFe® Scrum
Master, Certified Scrum Master, Professional Scrum
Master, and IATA Airline Marketing & International
Travel and Tourism.

**Leadership is not about position — it is about purpose,
service, and legacy.**

Through books, coaching, speaking, and leadership
development initiatives, Aaron's mission is to raise a new
generation of purpose-driven leaders who influence
organizations, communities, and nations.

CONNECT WITH AARON PREMPEH

Aaron Prempeh welcomes opportunities to connect with readers, leaders, organizations, and institutions who are passionate about leadership development, personal growth, and transformational impact.

For speaking engagements, leadership training, coaching programs, partnerships, or media inquiries, please reach out through the following channels.

Contact Information

Email:
aaronprempeh@gmail.com

Phone:
+1-614-843-0509

Location:
Iowa City, Iowa, USA

Official Websites

Personal Website
aaronprempeh.com

Author & Books
aaronprempehbooks.com

Purpose Givers Leadership Platform
purposegivers.co

Speaking, Coaching, and Leadership Development

Aaron Prempeh is available for:

- Leadership conferences and keynote speaking
- Corporate leadership training programs
- Church and ministry leadership development
- Executive and personal leadership coaching
- Youth and emerging leader mentorship programs

Organizations, universities, churches, and leadership institutions interested in hosting Aaron for speaking engagements, seminars, or training programs are encouraged to reach out via email.

Stay Connected

Follow Aaron's work, new book releases, leadership insights, and upcoming programs through his official websites and platforms.

Together, we can raise a generation of leaders who lead with purpose, integrity, and lasting impact.

Champion Remain

FINAL BRAND SIGNATURE

Leadership is not about position — it is about purpose, service, and legacy.

Champion Remain.

WHAT EVERY LEADER MUST KNOW

Aaron Prempeh

www.ingramcontent.com/pod-product-compliance
Lightning Source LLC
Chambersburg PA
CBHW031111160726
47991CB00004B/1331